Live to Tell

A Suicide Survivor's Struggle with Depression & Anxiety

Ben Schwipps &
Shelia Merkel

ISBN: 978-0692689011

*To those who are struggling to see the light
and the promise of a new day*

*To all of my friends and family who shared
time, thoughts and prayers towards my
recovery. I'll forever be in your gratitude.*

To Megan—I meant every word I ever said.

Contents

Acknowledgments..7
Introduction..9
Preface I..17
Preface II...22
1—Happiness Is a State of Mind..........24
2—Rebuilding the Happiness—The Story of a Girl...28
3—Decisions...33
4—Congratulations! ... I'm Sorry.........38
5—Pulling Up from the Nosedive.........45
6—Back to the Rocking Horse.............49
7—Damage Done...................................59
8—And So It Begins.............................68
9—Bending Ears until They Break.......76
10—Hope for Change............................81

11—Goodbye Is All We've Got Left to Say86
12—Dismantle. Repair........................96
13—"Hello." "Hey." 113
14—Xanadu 120
15—Dark Is a Place; Light Is the Way. 128
16—Don't Do What Ben Did............... 135
17—Suicide Warning Signs 140
18—Reach Out and Touch Someone .. 143
19—Ten Things Not to Say 149
20—Ripple Effects.............................. 155
21—The Phoenix Rises.......................158
A Request......................................161
Resources 162
About the Authors............................ 167
Shelia's Story of This Book............... 169

Acknowledgments

I want to personally thank my friend and co-author, Ben Schwipps, for having the courage to share his story. Rather than putting his head in the sand, he holds his head high and works to improve his life day by day and the lives of others he has touched through sharing his experience.

This book would not exist without the support of the Facebook community group of authors who self-publish. Daily inspiration, feedback, and sharing of ideas with a community of talented authors have made this journey a rewarding experience.

Introduction

I stood outside room 5237 on the fifth floor of the ICU section at UC Medical in Cincinnati. Hesitating, I took a deep breath and realized I had no clue what I was going to say. I didn't really have any fresh words of wisdom to share. I had no idea what condition he would be in. I had heard rumors on his prognosis and really didn't know what was true. I didn't know if he would recognize me.

When I walked in, I wondered if I was in the right room. I didn't recognize Ben at first. His head was shaved, and his face was swollen from the trauma of a recent surgery. He had large bump on his forehead. I had heard that the bullet was lodged in his sinus cavity and that there would be another surgery soon to remove that. His jaw was wired shut, and I didn't know if he could see me. He had a tube in his neck, but he was breathing on his own. There was a bandage underneath his chin, where, I assumed, lay the entry point for the bullet.

I walked to his bedside, and he immediately recognized me. He put his hand to his heart and thumped his fist to his chest. He wrote quickly on a small whiteboard on his lap, "I am so glad you came." I expected to see a defeated man, but instead I saw the resilience of the human spirit. I saw the old Ben that I knew. As I asked questions, he penned answers on the whiteboard.

"Ben, you have survived this for a reason. This was not your time to leave this earth. Your life will have new meaning. Your life may be different, but I see great things ahead of you. I think we should write a book. This is simply a miracle that you survived, and a book will be a great way that you can help and inspire others. There are millions of people out there who struggle with depression."

I rambled on for a few minutes. I wanted to give hope and assurance that things would work out. I knew he was struggling after going through a recent divorce, but I know everyone struggles with the ups and downs of life. I believed and wanted him to believe that life could and would get better and that he would find true happiness and success in his life.

As I left the hospital, the idea of writing a book never left me. The very next day I received an email from one of the newsletters I subscribe to and the topic of the article was on book writing, citing the reasons why you should write a book. The timing was surreal. I took this as a "sign," and I knew I would bring this idea to Ben again when he was more on the path to recovery.

Through Ben's personal story, the purpose of this book is give an inside view and account for what it is like to battle depression. This is an insider's perspective and not the view of a doctor or scholar who understands the science and treatment of depression and other mental illness disorders. This book is about breaking the rules and the social stigma around depression and suicide. We want to talk about it candidly, in a way that the everyday person can understand. I will warn you that some parts of the book are disturbing.

Ben's story is real, and the emotions are raw and very personal. This book will answer all the questions about why Ben took deliberate action to end his life late in the afternoon on July 18, 2015. This book will talk about the warning signs of suicide and specific tips on how to start a conversation with someone you fear is depressed and suicidal.

According to statistics from 2013, eight million Americans, 13% of the population, attempt suicide every year, and 18% of all college students seriously consider ending their lives. There are not many survivors that live to tell their stories. There is a population that has fleeting thoughts of ending their life, and there is then 6% that actually makes the attempt.

Only a person who has lived through this harrowing event can explain why they did it. No one really understands from the outside looking in. It is irrational to the vast majority of people. I will readily admit that even for me, the boss and friend looking at what Ben did, I totally missed all the warning signs that led to that night on Saturday, July 18.

I hired Ben in 2007 and worked with him over for over seven years. He worked as a key member of our operations team when we were building out a new line of business. He met my niece at work, and they later married. Ben became part of our extended family and a regular face at family gatherings.

What I always admired most about Ben was his smile and easygoing spirit, a very friendly guy, always upbeat. He was a strong asset to our team, a crucial cog in the wheel for building a service model designed to take care of customers. I needed someone who was passionate about customer service and who would go the extra mile. That was the Ben I knew, the guy with a spring in his step and a smile on his face.

After Ben's near death, I asked myself over and over, *What could I have done differently? How did I miss all the warning signs?* I saw and interacted with Ben every day. *How did I not see this coming?* Others at work were feeling the same guilt and regret over the incident. *Why did I not step in and intervene? Could I have done something to help? Why did I miss all the warning signs?*

This book presents Ben's personal story of his journey to coping with depression and how to go back to leading a joyful and happy life. We all want and deserve happiness in our lives. I represent the outsider looking in and am stepping in to help facilitate Ben's story. I will not pretend that I fully understand depression and the games the mind plays. I know a lot of people who battle depression, including some of my own family members. For me, working with Ben to tell his story is a way to help get his story out there and also learn more about depression along the way.

I do promise, however, that after reading this book and Ben's personal story, you will have a greater insight into depression and you will be able to better help someone in your life that is struggling with this disease. You will have more compassion and understanding, and you will be more confident to intervene and take action if you know someone who is threatening suicide or is heading down the rabbit hole. When someone gets so low, it is hard for them to get up by themselves—so you need to be there, if possible, and give that helping hand.

If you are a depressed individual, you may see yourself in this story and you will know that you are not alone in your fight. Ben will help you to see what others do not understand. Consider Ben to be your friend and guiding light. If Ben can help a few others, they will also providing healing to Ben.

Like anyone who battles with depression and even negative thoughts, healing and recovery are not an overnight process. We are not alone in this world for a reason, although for someone battling depression daily, it can feel like you are alone in your fight.

Take action today by downloading this book. There is no doubt in my mind that you will benefit by reading a personal account of Ben's story. In these pages you will find out why Ben pulled the trigger in his living room after making a phone call. You will find out what he wrote in his journal and about the suicide notes to his family and friends. You will find out all the things going on his life, the triggers and amplifiers that led up to the event. You may see yourself in the pages or have a greater understanding of what someone close to you is going through, or has gone through.

After reading this book, I guarantee that you will get to know Ben and will find out what a great guy he is and what a gift to the world he is. I think you will make a friend, and everyone needs a friend and supporter in their life.

Ben was the happy-go-lucky, normal guy to the outside world, but inside he was a broken man, teetering on the edge of the precipice. He pulled the trigger. He regretted it. He died. He was revived. He died again. He was revived for the second time. After the event, when he awoke in the hospital, he recalls a burning desire to make things right again. This book is Ben's attempt to make things right again. He genuinely wants to help others who are struggling, who are at the breaking point.

Thanks for reading about Ben's story and recommending this book to your network of friends. We are all on a journey together making our way in this world. We are here to lend a hand to help one another. Enjoy this read and then take action to reach out and help someone who might be struggling. You never know who is hurting inside and who is at the end of their rope ... literally.

—Shelia Merkel (Cincinnati, OH)

Preface I

My phone buzzed. Glancing down, I saw the text—*Did you hear about Ben?* My phone buzzed a few more times. It was very unusual to gets texts on a Sunday morning. I was in route to my yoga class in Clifton. *Ben* ... I wondered what happened. *A car accident?* Then I learned that Ben was shot the previous night. *What? Is this a joke? A gun accident? He probably hunted and had guns in the house.*

Rumor had it that he shot himself. No one seemed to know his status—if he was dead or alive. There was no word on his condition, other than that he was taken to University of Cincinnati Medical and was in their IC unit. Any gunshot wound to the head was never good. I imagined the worst.

I arrived at Modo Yoga, and, not really knowing what to do next, I decided to go on with the class and digest this information. I was at a loss. *Ben*

… I'd exchanged brief words with him on Friday. When the work day was over, he filed past my desk toward the door with a few others to start the weekend. *Hey, Shelia—Have a great weekend! You too, Ben!* He had a smile on face.

I went through the motions of the yoga practice like a robot. My thoughts were far away, thinking of Ben and his family. I thought of his two young sons, Ryan and Evan. His parents and family. I thought of Megan and her son, Hunter. This was devastating news to everyone who knew Ben. Tears streamed down my face. Fortunately the room was dimmed and heated to about 103 degrees. The tears mixed with the sweat dripping onto the mat, so no one noticed.

I thought back to the previous week at work. I knew that Megan had recently filed for a divorce and that Ben was taking it hard. Everyone knows that a divorce can be gut-wrenching and all the emotions that go along with it will take the wind out of your sails. This was not all that unusual. He'd lost a bit a weight, had taken a vacation day here and there to work through everything. While at work, he'd seemed totally focused and performed well.

Something was wrong with the picture. *Why did I not see any warning signs?* I knew of the pending divorce. *Could I have intervened somehow and prevented this?* I should have made more of an effort to be a friend and lend an ear if he needed. On the other hand, I know divorce is so personal, and I really didn't want to interfere or take sides. I wanted the best for both Ben and Megan. Divorce is such a personal decision.

Ben and I had talked about the divorce casually a few weeks prior but he'd sounded normal and sane. He didn't want his marriage to end. He wanted things to work out with Megan. Hunter was like a son to Ben, and I had always thought they all made a great family. His state of mind seemed totally normal for anyone going through some personal upheaval. I'd always assured him, *Things will get better. Hang in there.*

Still, something was wrong with the picture. Divorce does not lead people to put a gun to their head ... normally. I realized that I didn't know the rest of the story. I knew that he was not where he wanted to be in his career. Financial problems put an extra strain on the marriage. Still there was something else that triggered this event. After the class I called my Mom and Dad's house. Their house is like grand central station—the place to go for lunch to connect with family, have a delicious home-cooked meal, and find out the latest news about relatives and friends.

Dad answered the phone and had also heard about Ben, but they did not have any information other than he was shot and was at UC Medical. I decided to call Ben's mother next. I didn't know Ben's parents personally, but I had met them briefly at Ben and Megan's wedding reception a few years back.

Not knowing what to say, I expressed my concern and asked about Ben's condition. I learned that he was alive and had gone through a touch and go situation the previous night. There were several times where they almost lost him. The family did not know the extent of his injuries. They did not know if he would be able to see or speak or if there would be brain damage. They were going to meet with the doctor that afternoon to understand the extent of his injuries.

I recall being amazed with Ben's mother's strength in taking control and talking about the situation. I put myself in her shoes, said a quick prayer for her strength, and tried to take some mental notes with the information she was sharing. I knew it was a wait-and-see situation from there. All we could do was pray and hope for the best.

Let's rewind the clock a bit. I am turning the story over to Ben so that he can tell you about the events in his life that led up to that tragic summer evening in July.

I am grateful that he lived to tell his story.

Preface II

We can let circumstances rule us, or we can take charge and rule our lives from within.
—E.N.

Lost.

That's basically how I felt inside. One of the most horrible things in the world is to have the feeling of being lost. No, I'm not talking about taking a wrong turn on the interstate and ending up in the wrong part of town but rather, emotionally, physically, and, ultimately mentally—lost. For some, it's due to the loss of a loved one, a child moving out, the changing of a lifestyle due to a job or career change. For me, however, it was a combination of all of the above. The hideous "perfect storm."

This is my story of dealing with depression, suicide, and, finally, the coping and goal-setting determination of conquering this ghastly sickness. I hope it serves as either an inspiration or just an outline of how a person like me went from great to bad to worse, and is on the way back to being the person I wanted to be.

I had some assistance along the way from counselors, doctors, friends, and family, but I credit most of my success to my own self-determination and the realization that I was getting better and wanted to be better again. You have to want to be better, and that is often a hard battle to realize needs fighting.

Best of luck in your journey, and know that you are never alone.

1—Happiness Is a State of Mind

At the age of 23, I married my first wife. We had dated for almost five years, and we figured it was time. We both had good jobs and career paths, stable incomes, and, above all, goals for a future. Like any marriage, there were ups and downs, but having dated for those five years, we'd already worked through many of thc "growing pains" as a couple. As time went on, there were changes of jobs, career paths, income, houses, and also the addition of two wonderful children.

Granted, those are things that seem pretty normal in any marriage to this point, but those changes also carried a downside—stress—one of the many words I consider an "ugly word," as it can be the hairline fracture that brings down the castle wall. So, after nine years of marriage, we ended in divorce. The stresses of income, financial lifestyle, and job changes were the culprit.

At times, we were fine, but most other times our house resembled a scene from *The Sopranos.* Nothing that I cared to live with, nor did she. That's when we realized it was time to go our separate ways.

The hardest part was leaving everything that I'd worked hard for and grown accustomed to in my young-adult life. Not only was I leaving a very nice home, cars, and personal belongings, I was losing the privilege of seeing my kids grow up daily before my very eyes. Guilt over this crept in, but what was done was done. What I didn't realize was that for me, that guilt brought along a friend to my party, and its name was DEPRESSION.

Looking back, I can almost remember the day that I realized that something wasn't right. I went to work, enjoyed my job, but felt the hole that happiness once occupied. After seeing one of many ads on television about medication for treatment of anxiety and depression, I made the call to my personal physician to schedule a checkup and discuss what I thought might be the case.

After talking to the doctor about it more, it was determined that my symptoms were textbook for depression—loss of interest in daily activities, loss of motivation, sleep changes, anger, sadness, and self-loathing. These are things that normally I had no problems with.

Hearing that I had a "sickness" that to this point I'd thought existed only on commercials was a bit disturbing in its own right. My doctor assured me that it was a very common thing and very treatable. I knew of no one personally that had suffered from it, as it's nothing that really got discussed amongst my friends. I had more than a case of the blues, which I'd originally thought might have been the case.

I was placed on a low-grade dose of medication to begin the combat and followed up regularly with my physician to monitor problems and/or progress. After what seemed like a long time, I began feeling the difference in my daily life. I had more energy, more of a drive to accomplish much-needed goals, and fewer feelings of despair.

I didn't do anything but rely on the medicine and bury myself in work, which seemed to be my only constant at the time when I wasn't spending time with my kids. All seemed to be okay, but down deep—I craved more. I was ready to begin a new chapter, a rebuild of sorts, and soon I'd find it.

Ben's Insights

As mentioned right above, GOALS are a must. When depression is the case, a person often finds no ambition to accomplish anything but get up, do what has to be done with minimal effort, and then go back to bed. Personal achievements seem nonexistent and not important. Without goals, every day is just another day, and the mountain you are trying to climb remains a mountain rather than being reduced to a mole hill.

I realized that medicine only helps one part of the equation. It is critical to find a way to deal with life's pains and injuries and the source of the pain instead of just burying oneself in work and other distractions. It is best to seek out therapy and not just rely on medicine. If the underlying issue is not solved, it can set someone up for the downward spiral that I am going to share with you.

2—Rebuilding the Happiness—The Story of a Girl

A couple of months after my divorce, I was promoted at work to the job I had coveted since my first days of being hired. I moved up! I did it! I was driving an hour and a half each way for the job because I had changed locations, but that didn't matter. I had the job! I felt a lot of despair literally melt when I got the offer and acceptance letter. I still have that email to this day.

Everyone I worked with was very happy for me, as was my family. The hard work I had used as a coping method (which many often use, as it serves as a wonderful distraction of sorts) had paid off, and I felt a pull away from the grasp of my depression. Truthfully, it was the beginning of what I thought was my victory dance over being sick and was only eclipsed by the relationship I soon started with the love of my life.

It all started at a copy machine. I was still at my old position, still married, but going through the beginnings of the divorce, and she was a temp in another department. I found myself standing behind someone I had never met before, and I had been employed for about a year at that time and felt I knew just about everyone in the office.

I said the customary "hello" when she finally turned my way and was greeted with a very unenthusiastic "hey". It wasn't love at first sight, but little did I realize at the time, I had just had an exchange with the woman I would eventually realize was my soul mate.

After a couple of months and the finalization of my divorce, I brought myself to the idea that I ought to try to talk to her more. We'd had several conversations as time went on since we worked in parallel departments, but nothing more than just casual conversations. I learned a lot about her, and she about me. I finally got the courage to ask her on a date, and, to my surprise, she accepted. My first date in 14 years!

Nervous and anxious were understatements. It was not a depression kind of anxiety, where a person would feel sad over the loss of a previous relationship and the guilt of starting perhaps a new one. This was, instead, anxiety of an entirely different kind.

We had set the date for a Saturday night, but when Friday came along, I was so anxious to see her that I asked her impromptu for a date for that evening as well. She surprisingly accepted on short notice and the weekend began.

To this point, I had covered and buried my pain and depression with dedication to my new job, spending the time I had with my kids in positive ways and trying to pick up old hobbies that would help occupy free time. These were excellent "coping mechanisms" to accompany the medication I was still taking. It was working because I was happy.

Megan and I hit it off, and, within a few short weeks, I was in love. Hand to God, I had never been happier in my life. If someone were to have told me I was depressed at that time, they would've been dismissed as a liar. It was at this point I decided to take myself off of the medication. I had life by the horns after all, right? Depression surely couldn't be a problem anymore, right?

WRONG.

Life, as it does, happens. Within a couple of months, there were financial aftermaths to deal with regarding my divorce that came up along the way and caused stresses, but we overcame most of them. We had many ups and downs, and I felt depression gaining on me once again. About this time, I noticed my drinking picked up substantially.

Thankfully, with Megan's urging, I revisited my doctor, who scolded me for going off the medication, even though I had told him of my newfound happiness. He didn't discount or take away from my feelings, but informed me that while the battle with this sickness can be won, it takes more time and sometimes never goes away. He advised me to get back on the medications, even recommending a different type.

After the typical first weeks or so, I could feel the difference, and I was back on track. Life, once again, continued to be a happy place to be for me.

Ben's Insights

Earlier in this chapter, I made mention of "coping mechanisms." These are absolutely essential to combating depression and anxiety. For some, it's exercise, such as yoga or boxing, aromatherapy, spending time with family and friends, donating time to charity, knitting, etc. Anything that keeps one's mind from having to focus on the pressure of the situation at hand and can provide a sense of "vacation for your emotions" is an example of a coping mechanism. For me, falling in love was a great thing.

While coping mechanisms are helpful, please be aware that temporary mood boosts don't resolve the deep inner pain. When new stresses surfaces, the old pain rears up again. I may sound like a broken record, but seek out therapy and do not just rely on typical coping patterns. Therapy will help shift a person from being very vulnerable to being more resilient in dealing with life's challenges.

3—Decisions

With life going well and seeming to consistently fire on all cylinders, I felt confident to take the next step in my relationship with Megan. She continued to make me the happiest man alive. Every morning when I took my medication, I felt like it was a waste of time, as there was nothing that could possibly make a bigger difference than she could, but I kept with it per the good doctor's orders.

I asked my two boys, Ryan and Evan and her son, Hunter one morning what they would think about me asking Megan to become my wife. The three boys had become quite bonded during the every-other-weekend and once-a-week rotation I had established, and my sons also liked Megan a lot. She treated them well, and, even though there was a difference in the ages of our children, they got along well. I was answered with an excited, "YES, DAD!" Step one done.

Everyone always says that kids are resilient and can roll with about anything. While this is true with some things, it can be very different with others. Having been divorced almost a year, I was asking my children to basically realize that their mom and dad were moving on and that they were going to have to accept (or not accept, potentially) a step-parent into their lives. To some, this can trigger an emotionally depressing situation, but thankfully in my case, it was the opposite for them.

Continuing in the same vein of wanting to do things "right" this time, I knew I wanted to ask for permission to marry the love of my life. Unfortunately, Megan's father had passed away about two years prior to our meeting, something about which I am certain she carries a certain degree of sadness and sense of loss.

Megan comes from a wonderful family. A family that looks out for one another and that helped her and her son out many times since her father passed. Her uncle, in particular, became a sort of father figure to her and her son. It was he whom I asked for permission, and I was granted that permission with a smile. It was official. I was going to ask Megan to marry me.

Making a life-changing decision like this did cause me a lot of uncertainty though, as I was unsure how my ex-wife would handle the idea of the boys' officially having a step-parent. I was unsure if financially I was able to provide for a new family of five, rather than just the three I was now used to. Megan and I still worked together at the same place, but finances can be the nail in the road that blows the tire of happiness (as I'd experienced previously), and I didn't want to go through that ever again.

After a couple of weeks weighing all the possible problems and solutions of my decision, not only for me, but for her, we decided to get married. I had already purchased the most beautiful ring I'd ever seen and was ready to place it on the finger of the woman I loved.

On a gorgeous, mid-summer day, I surprised her by dropping to one knee and asking her to be mine forever. As hoped for, she said yes. The word "depression" did not exist at that point. My path to happiness had come full circle. I had the job, the family, and now the woman of my dreams.

With that idea, I went off my meds once again and did okay for awhile, as I was on a euphoric high of being in love and from career success.

Sure, there were very minor ups and downs, but nothing that I chalked up to more than adjusting to the idea that two were going to become one in many ways.

We wed a few months later in a very minimalistic ceremony and enjoyed a reception at the home of one of her family members. To see many joyous and smiling people, to be welcomed into a wonderful family, along with our very happy children, was awesome. It was a great day. Depression ... never heard of it.

Ben's Insights

It is important to realize that depression and anxiety affect more than just adults. Children are definitely not immune to this sickness, either. It is important to discuss situations and feelings with them, and seek treatment if suspicious of symptoms. Children who have a family history of anxiety and depression are more likely to experience it themselves.

Also, there are many different medications for many different types of depression and severity levels. These medicines, coupled with therapy, can be an effective way to deal with circumstances and symptoms. Medications may take trial and error to dial in the proper treatment plan and dosage, and a physician can determine the best plan with a consultation. It is important to follow all instructions and commit to the medicine in order to make a difference. With your physician's help, medicine will make a difference, and it is advisable to consult with them if you decide to stop the medication as well. Something I didn't do.

4—Congratulations! ... I'm Sorry

After marrying Megan, life continued to be fine. Our nuclear family seemed to be doing well, not without the fair share of stresses. Kids squabble. Schedules get hectic. Dollars turn into dimes, and needs and situations are always changing. We rolled with the punches, dealt with pressures, and, like anyone battling over anything that they believed in, we hung on with white knuckles and bare teeth, coming out okay.

Work continued to be good for us both, and we eventually decided to make the move from her smaller home to a larger one. We found a home in a small, neighboring town that fit our needs perfectly. We discussed and discussed it, and then decided to go for it. We made arrangements to place her home for sale once we negotiated for the new home, and the adventure was on its way!

Of course with excitement comes anxiety, something that we BOTH had. Overriding our anxiety, we put our efforts into our work, preparations for the potential move, and dealing with life on a day-to-day level. We overhauled several things on the home to make it more marketable, and our efforts paid off.

We had an offer within two weeks of the house being on the market, and it was sold in little over a month. We did it! The kids were super excited, as they would each have their own room (not to mention a bathroom they could call their own) and the wonder of moving to a new place.

As for Megan and me, we also embraced it with excitement, as it was something we always told ourselves we wanted. The finances were in order, our jobs secure, and our marriage was strong as ever. We were standing on the proverbial solid ground that one needs in order to make a decision such as this.

The occupancy agreement was that we were to hand over the keys to the buyer in 14 days from the closing day. We had been somewhat planning for this since the offer had been accepted, but the new home had some finishing touches that were needed, so the weight of a timeline became pretty heavy.

We worked full-time at our jobs during the day, came home, inhaled food, and made trips to the new home to paint, take loads of belongings over, and ready the home for new carpeting. We managed to make the move in just a few days, which were celebrated with several cold beers, smiles, and very sound nights of sleep.

Ironically, within a week of our move, I received a call from my manager, who was also the Senior Vice President of our division. While it wasn't uncommon for us to talk many evenings on occasion about fishing, Las Vegas, and old cars, all of which we shared a passion for, this call was different.

He called to talk about work and the possibility of some potential changes that the company might be looking to make "sometime in the future." Nothing was conveyed in any kind of negative way, as it was just small talk. During our chat, I told him of our new home purchase and our excitement for what we'd just accomplished.

I sensed a nervous joy in his voice but didn't think anything about it. I went to bed, enjoying the fact that life had finally calmed down from the move, the kids were doing great, and I loved my wife. Sleep came easy.

Then, a month later, the call came.

While at my desk one afternoon, my coworker and I were summoned to one of the meeting rooms for a conference call with our manager. When we walked into the room and saw our human resources representative seated already, my heart immediately raced. What had I done? What did this mean for the company? Was I in trouble overall?

I seated myself and watched nervously as she dialed the telephone number for my manager. Once we had him on the phone, it was explained that our company had decided to move him from one of our offices to another and had decided to centralize all of our sales and marketing team (to which I belonged) to Houston, Texas.

It might as well have been to Mars, as there was just as much chance of me going there as there was to Houston, Texas. I'm not sure if my jaw hit the ground or not. I'm not even sure I took a breath. I just remember the feeling that my dream job that I'd based a lot of happiness, dedication, financial decisions, and pride on was going away (unless I wanted to make the move to keep it).

We were given the option of taking a severance, moving with the company, or applying for another position within the company. There was an apology about the situation and then the resonating click of the phone as the call came to an end. "Exhale" is all I remember thinking to myself. That—and I was ready for a stiff drink.

When I'd learned of the meeting, I'd told Megan about it, but neither of us had expected anything like this to occur. When I walked out of the meeting, I remember going to her desk, accompanying her on her break, and telling her the news.

I told her of the terms that were laid out for me, and it was unanimously and immediately decided that the move was not an option, nor was severance. I decided that I would pursue something within the company, hoping that something would come up.

Anxiety and depression ramped back into full view in my rearview mirror, and I'm sure hers as well. Within a short time, we found ourselves arguing and stressing about the hows and whats we were going to do.

Arguing was something that she and I rarely did. Up to this point, true arguments with Megan could be counted on one hand, and we were going on almost four years of being together. That's a pretty good average by anyone's measure.

This stress caused cracks in the relationship that I once considered stronger than anything. The search immediately began for new positions, and time was ticking. The ticking resembled that of a knock at the door. The door was opened, and in walked the return of the twins, also known as depression and anxiety.

Ben's Insights

Anxiety symptoms include constant worry, insomnia, difficulty concentrating, and more, lasting for several months. According to The Huffington Post, some of the top reasons for anxiety include money woes, children, not being able to predict the future (uncertainty), being alone, death, meeting new people, and several others. Many people experience mild anxiety over these things from time to time, but if the feelings last for more than six months, it is advised to contact your doctor or physician immediately.

5—Pulling Up from the Nosedive

About a month after the original call, my manager called and said he might have an option for me. In development was a new group that was going to focus on internal employees that could help generate sales for one of our other divisions. While it sounded interesting, I had my reservations as I knew nothing really about the subject matter. I'd worked for almost five years in the company alongside this department but knew nothing really about it.

Regardless, I was immediately responsive to the idea and enthusiastic that there was something there for me. Granted, I could have cast resumes out to other places, but why? I loved the company, loved what I did, and, hey, I got to work with my wife. I had no intentions of going anywhere. I was still unsure about the job though, as nobody likes to be assumed an expert under high expectations and then to turn out to be a failure. Nervousness set in, but the need was met. I had a job to go to, and that itself eased the tension, for the present at least.

As the day got closer for me to end one job and start another, I felt a growing pressure inside. The sadness of closing a familiar and loved chapter of my life and beginning a new and slightly confusing one really started to sink in. I recall having an anxiety attack one evening at home over it, and my wife took me to our local urgent care to ensure it wasn't anything major. I was that nervous.

Through all of this though, I remember my first day in the department when I was welcomed aboard by the other members of the team. I knew I was in good company, and they were willing to bring me up to speed as quickly as they could.

The products were different, and I think that mentally, I just couldn't grasp it because I was so programmed with previous knowledge of our other products that it made it hard to comprehend.

For the very first time in my life, I actually had the sense that my job performance was going to cost me the job. I missed the type and line of business that I'd previously done, so the search began once again to find my passion. At least I had an income to fall back on in the meantime.

I lasted a total of six months at that position, and then an opportunity outside the company arose, introducing a whole new set of complexities into my cracking castle. Financial stress had been kept at bay during that time, but performance anxiety was always a factor.

I managed to use almost three weeks of vacation while working at this position, something I hadn't ever done before. Previously, I never took much time off, as I loved my job. However, this time it was different.

I began drinking more heavily during this time. Initially, I had beers almost every night, typically with friends. We had wonderful neighbors that we hung out with quite a bit, and our kids were all close in age. It wasn't anything for us to be found at one another's homes watching our children run around like wild children playing while we enjoyed drinks and playing cards. It was a great group. But as time passed, I found myself a lot more often--alone.

When I was approached about a potential job outside the company, I consulted with my neighbor, Joel, who was a director of a sales center. I explained to him the role I was contemplating, and he and I discussed numerous pros and cons of taking such a position that involved commission-based income.

I had the confidence in myself, but I just needed to make the sale. Eventually, I left my company and branched out to the new role. It turned out to be a move that I would later regret. Enter the twins, once again. This time they came to take no prisoners. Their wrath involved not only me, but my family. The tailspin had begun.

Ben's Insights

Many physicians recommend avoiding alcohol while seeking treatment for depression, as it can make many antidepressant medications ineffective. Many folks can get by with a simple drink to take the edge off of anxiety, but for someone with depression, it can make problems worse.

People who are depressed and drink too much have more frequent and severe episodes of depression, and they are more likely to think about suicide. More on this to come.

6—Back to the Rocking Horse

After much discussion with Megan about my unhappiness with the new role I had assumed within the company, I decided that I would further pursue the opportunity outside the company. It was something along the vein of what I had done before, but with more of an emphasis on sales.

It sounded exciting, and the financial possibilities, if successful, were vast. I bit the hook that was baited with dollar bills and turned in a notice to the company that I had given over five years of my life to, the place where I'd met and fallen in love with my wife, the place made up of people whom I considered family.

It was an uneasy feeling to walk out of that building for the last time after turning in my key. Granted, Megan was secure in her job, and we were thankful for that. Still, mine was not guaranteed, but I had confidence that if I loved what I was doing again, the success would come.

The new position was no longer a convenient fifteen minutes from home, but rather an hour and a half of city and interstate traffic each way. Construction and accidents were the norm, and I found myself leaving before the kids got up and getting home just in time to grab a dinner plate and assist with homework before having to ensure showers and teeth were done and tuck them in.

The job itself was as described. It was definitely a sales-oriented one, with an emphasis in juggling many chainsaws in the form of numerous company relationships and product knowledge that needed to be called upon at any given time. I went from being a jack of all trades to a master of none, per se.

I worked at the new position for approximately 90 days. The first month was good and flew by, as I considered it the newlywed phase of the job. The drive was not much of a factor, and the hours spent studying the new materials and learning the ropes were no problem. I rolled with the punches.

By the second month, the reality of the drive became more obvious, the pressure began to climb regarding sales production, and it got a little more stressful. Still, I was making progress, but not nearly as fast as I had hoped or as quickly as I was told I would.

By the third month, the drive had taken a toll on me to the point that I dreaded putting the key in the car each morning, dreaded making the required 80–100 cold calls a day to outside agents and pitching a sales presentation only to get told to "take them off the list" numerous times.

I had good phone etiquette, but the audience that I was reaching out to had heard it all before. I was no different. The production expectations were still there, but the sales weren't. Each day I required more and more self-motivation not to call into work, wishing I had those three weeks of time off again that I previously had with the other role to use. Sadly, I didn't.

The stress followed me home each night, as I found it increasingly hard to leave it at the desk at work. I found myself arguing with Megan more, as she had stresses of her own. Our kids were doing well in school, but juggling busy schedules at work and at home, not to mention other activities (I was also a volunteer firefighter) left little time each evening to connect with each other and unwind.

Weekends were coveted and too short. Next thing you know, it was Monday and the car key once again had to find its way into the ignition, signaling another long commute to a job that was considered a failed experiment in my eyes.

Meanwhile, Megan still worked at the same place as before and was always getting asked how I was getting along with my new job. Being a person who isn't known for mincing words, she often told people the truth about how it was going for us. One day, while talking to a coworker in the compliance department, she shared the situation. I'd had a good relationship with this department, and the respect was mutual.

As it turned out, they were in the process of creating a new position and would soon seek approval to post for it. She was urged to tell me about it, which she did, and I immediately got excited. The opportunity to "come back home" and work with the same department (although in a slightly different role) appealed to me. To work once again in the same building as my wife and reconnect with coworkers that were like extended family was just what I was looking for, so my hopes began to climb.

I was told that it might be a month or so before the position and budget were approved for the new job, but if I could get back into the company via another position, they would simply draft me from there. I contacted the director of my old department, advised her of the situation I was working on, and she was more than happy to assist.

Once she and I completed the negotiations, I put the key in the ignition one last time and made the commute to the big city with a smile on my face and a formal two-week notice in my hand. As each mile passed, I felt less and less pressure and stress, and could envision happiness returning anytime soon.

While there was a sense of security about going back to where it all began, it wasn't without a cost. I'd left the company making substantially more than I was coming back to. To be exact, I had agreed to a 51% decrease in pay, but, after much debate, Megan and I took solace in the fact that it was to be short-term until the new job came to fruition.

Was this a gamble? Sure. Nothing in life is guaranteed. We were no strangers at this point to living paycheck to paycheck (something that once again created numerous cracks), but we were surviving, God knows how. Each night after my first month back, we went to bed with heads on pillows, hoping to hear good news the next day.

Stress, anxiety, and depression were all living with us, full-time at this point, so much that it was costing us much more than just money. It was taking an emotional toll. I felt it, Megan felt it, and I can't help but think that our kids felt the stress as well.

We'd always had nice things, but as the time ticked by waiting for the new role and the income it carried with it, we found ourselves getting behind. We sold off things we could do without to alleviate payments and to cover bills and expenses here and there, but soon paychecks being spent before they were even in the account became the norm.

On top of all this, the month or so that I found myself waiting for the new position turned into many months.

One evening while talking to our neighbor Joel, Megan was presented with an opportunity of her own. They were creating a position that required a person to monitor sales agents and manage call center flow.

Knowing that she would be working with our neighbor was something that was considered a good thing, as he seemed to enjoy his job. The company was sound, reputable, and the position was something she could easily handle. She interviewed for the job, landed it, and was making more money than she had previously.

She enjoyed the new responsibility; however, it came with a downside. Once again, a city and interstate commute to work was required that involved early mornings and late evenings. Still, her happiness with the new job, the fact that the kids were still able to be taken care of each morning and night by me, and the additional income were worth it.

She brought stresses home with her, but they were often self-imposed, as she wanted to be the best at what she did. It didn't get to her much, but it was still present. Meanwhile, I was still in a holding pattern for the new job, and I was quickly approaching the six-month mark. After numerous calls, emails, and inquiries about it, I was told the company decided to take a different approach as to the candidate's qualifications. They would go on to outsource much of the work with the remaining work being distributed to the existing department.

The position I had been told about died on the vine, and I saw nothing but darkness in the tunnel. I remember the drive home that night as a quiet one, and I was thankful that there was cold beer in our refrigerator and that Megan still had an hour before she'd be home to share my news too.

It was a conversation that led to tears, feelings of helplessness, and despair. I remember feeling as though I were the conductor of a train going off the track and I was taking my family along for the ride. The situation not only affected me personally, but my entire family.

That evening while making supper, I opened the cabinet to retrieve dinner plates. I saw my medication sitting there and realized that it might be just what I needed. It had been awhile since I'd taken it consistently, and I was hoping that my body might still recognize its benefits and kick start back into action.

Unfortunately, medication like this is not like taking an aspirin for a headache. It doesn't come to the rescue within twenty minutes or so, and requires consistent doses to get back in your system and be effective. All are things I knew but figured I'd try anyway.

For the first time in my relationship with Megan, I could sense that being in love was starting to become something that might not be enough.

Ben's Insights

Money is the root of all evil—as the old saying goes. While it's easy to subscribe to this theory, it's not entirely true. The ability to deal with money is a learned thing, and if done correctly, can actually result in an entirely different perspective.

Financial stress is considered to be the number one trigger for marital problems in the world. Stress, depression, and anxiety are often participants in this factor and are commonly cited as being experienced by those going through said problems.

Counseling is advised if possible and is readily available by doing a yellow pages or Internet search. Financial and marriage counseling can be a great resource and, coupled with treatment for depression and/or anxiety disorders (if present), often can solve many problems before they escalate.

Never give up. Never.

7—Damage Done

I never was much in the financial management department. I only wanted to know if we had money, but when times got tough, I started to not ask. Megan was vigilant in making sure our bills were always something we were aware of, but handling our finances was much like reading a chapter in a sad novel every time she opened the checkbook.

It led to many arguments, but we always managed to financially pull our feet out of the fire in the end, albeit barely.

Every once in awhile, if we found ourselves with a surplus in the budget, I managed to somehow spend it. Like Jack with his valuable cow, I ended up trading it for magic beans in the form of something stupid, rather than paying down bills, making extra payments, or, in other words, doing the responsible thing.

The last straw for this was when I made a drunken purchase on eBay. One evening while enjoying several glasses of wine, I visited the site and browsed through memories of my childhood in the form a hobby I once loved, R/C vehicles. I placed a rather high bid on one that I was certain would be eclipsed and went on with life for the next few days.

As the auction drew to a close, a pop-up on my phone appeared one morning, stating that my auction would be ending soon and I was the high bidder. I was in the bathroom getting ready, and I immediately began to get nervous.

Surely there was no way I would win this, and there was surely no way I had the extra funds to pull it off. I watched all that day as the auction ticked down, and while several bidders came close, nobody defeated me.

It ended with me being the winner, and I immediately had a sense of excitement and dread. I calculated in my head ways to which I could "rob Peter to pay Paul" until the next paycheck. I had just sold an automobile and made a few hundred dollars of profit, so I thought, "Why not?"

I clicked the payment button and, figuring it would be easier to ask for forgiveness rather than permission, completed the sale and went to work.

The next morning, I went down to make coffee and found a note from Megan, thanking me for once again f*cking us financially and causing stress in our marriage. Like a hawk, she had seen online in our account that the money had been spent on a purchase.

As it would turn out, Megan was planning on using those funds to pay on a credit card that she carried that hadn't seen a payment for a couple of months because we'd needed the funds for other things (groceries, house payment, etc.).

I blew the funds on magic beans, putting what would be the final nail in the coffin of our marriage. Things were very different after that. I tried to explain the situation, but I was up against the cold, hard fact that she was trying to be responsible and I was trying to convince her to forgive a very irresponsible thing.

I once again forced stress and anxiety into our lives, and, this time, the damage was done. About a week after the purchase was made, I found myself in the hospital due to pancreatitis, which was likely caused by alcohol.

I spent almost a week in the hospital, leaving Megan to do all the duties of getting the kids ready for school, picking them up on time, and handling all homework duties. She was a one-person machine that was already coming apart at the seams, and it was becoming more and more obvious.

When I finally returned home from the hospital, little was I aware that she had begun researching a divorce. I knew things were different in her attitudes, but she always carried a poker face. Stress didn't go away, even after I turned around, resold the eBay item, and got the money back.

I had proven that our priorities were apparently very different. Crisis mode for her meant something entirely different to me. She took comfort in buckling down and seeing the money either stay in our account or go towards something that would eventually lead to further comfort, whereas I found comfort in spending money.

It's not uncommon behavior in people who are depressed, as the feeling of being able to buy something provides a short-lived happiness. In my case, it led to misery. Depression always found a way to win.

A week or two later, I came down after tucking the kids into bed to find Megan crying on the couch. To this point, I'd only seen Megan cry about three times, always about missing her father. This time, she was sobbing for a different reason. I recall asking her why she had tears as I sat down adjacent to her on the couch.

I'll never forget the look in her tired eyes as she told me she was done. She admitted that she could go no further because the stress of living like this another day would certainly give her a heart attack. She was absolutely genuine when she said those words, to which I replied that we'd be okay.

She shook her head, and I knew then and there that my commonly used phrase had run its course. She no longer believed me and, even worse, no longer believed *in* me. I asked her what she meant by "being done," and the words she spoke hit me like a bag of hammers to the chest—she wanted a divorce.

She had researched and found an attorney already who was on retainer, and she was going to move out. The process was underway, and there was no miraculous save to be made this time. Somewhere along the way, I'd pulled my last rabbit out of my hat, and she had no chances left to give me.

I know she genuinely loved me, as it pained her to tell me the news, but somewhere along the line she stopped caring for someone who didn't care about doing the right thing. I had single-handedly made numerous decisions that tore us apart.

I begged, I groveled, I promised change, and I cried, urging her to reconsider. All of which was sincere, but as it was, I didn't have a plan in mind to be able to pull it off fast enough. There was, once again, a rumbling of a new job opening within the company on the horizon, but in that arena, I was once bitten and twice shy.

I'd hung my hat on hope one too many times, and it led to where we were. "You can't pay bills with promises" was a thought I had as I went to bed that night. I likely didn't get much sleep that night, if any at all.

I remember the next day when I caught Megan before she went to work, I saw in her eyes the look of determination. She remembered everything from the night before, and I could tell that it wasn't just something that went away after a night of sleep. I called in to work and used a personal day, as I was in no shape to deal with the responsibility of giving any accurate information to anyone that needed it.

Crying all day, I immediately felt depression and anxiety crashing into me like waves on a beach, each one taking more and more out of me with each moment. This was really happening, and I all I wanted to do was wake up from what I was hoping was simply a terrible dream. This time, unfortunately, I was wide awake already.

The following weekend, Megan and her son moved out. We were amicable during the days leading to this, as I always tried to talk to her and plead to her forgiving side. Sadly, it didn't work. After the last load was put into her car, she pulled out of the drive for what was to be the last time as residents there. They were gone.

I was alone. Not entirely, as I still had my son, Ryan, living with me. He was at the time though at his mother's house for the weekend and would be home within a couple of hours.

During that timeframe, I curled in a ball and cried like never before. Depression had assumed the conductor's seat on my previously-mentioned train ride off the tracks, and I was helpless to do anything but close my eyes, hang on for dear life, and beg for it to stop.

Ben's Insights

Without seeing a physician and discussing your symptoms, admitting that you have a serious problem like depression is much like an alcoholic admitting they have a drinking problem. It's that difficult.

It can be a hard step, carrying its own stigma from others. As with alcoholism, looking in the mirror each day wondering how you're going to make it through is a common feeling for someone suffering from depression.

Once you get a handle on it and realize that what you're doing isn't working, it's time to call in the experts.

Prolonging an effective treatment plan will snowball into other aspects of your life, ultimately affecting family, work, and financial and personal areas. As I learned, sometimes the depression is caught too late.

8—And So It Begins

The next few weeks were a blur. To say I remember them accurately would be an outright lie. I do, however, know that I cried every day and fell even further into the depths of my depression.

I became less of a father to my children, more distracted at work, and more distant from the world. I tried, often unsuccessfully, to talk to Megan. She wanted no part of it, which was hard to accept. She needed her space to digest all that had and was happening, but I wasn't prepared to give that.

She was, after all, my best friend, and I had never imagined a life without her in it. Rejection is something that most find hard to accept, and I certainly was no different. It crushed me to hear the voicemail recording every time I would call or not to receive a return text. Thoughts raced through my mind about what she was doing, who she was with, and where she was. It was all-consuming.

During this time, I had effectively secluded myself from friends and family. Isolation only perpetuates and prolongs depression—trust me, I know.

In an effort to seek help, I made an appointment with my doctor, who kept me on the same medication; however, she increased the dosage to the maximum. I was taking double the dose I had previously been prescribed, and, after a week or two, I could barely tell the difference. It seemed that every day had challenges, and I was failing at them all.

One morning after placing Ryan on the bus, I remember sitting on my front porch step and just taking in the peace and quiet, but deep in thought of how I was going to make it through another day. My neighbor Joel, on his way to work, saw me sitting there and stopped in. Our friends were aware of what had been going on, especially Joel, who still worked with Megan.

He came inside and spent an hour talking me off my ledge for the moment. He outlined the many things I could and should do to try to move past the pain I was feeling, and while they made sense, I wasn't ready.

It was all too fresh and new for me to be ready to do that. I knew what I wanted, but I couldn't have it. Despair, hopelessness, and worthlessness were constant companions of mine, and I hated it.

The following weekend was Easter weekend. It was to be the first holiday that I would be spending away from my wife and in recent years had become one of my favorites. Her family has a tradition of spending it together, and, after attending many of them with them and her, I missed it. I not only lost my wife, but the family that came with her. I was very much on the outside looking in.

That day, I made my first attempt at suicide.

I went to the garage, started the car, and went back inside. After cutting a garden hose into pieces of the appropriate lengths, I secured them to the exhaust outlets of the car and routed them to the inside of the car. I carefully sealed the windows, door edges, and any possible areas where fresh air could diminish the effects of what I wanted to accomplish.

I took an undisclosed amount of pain pills, muscle relaxers, and a few sleep aids for good measure. Having researched a homemade concoction for an airborne poison, I came up with a mixture of bleach and vinegar, which destroys oxygen and causes lung damage upon inhalation.

I made a batch of this, placed it on the floorboard of the car, and went back inside once again. As quickly as I could, I drank the last six beers I had in the refrigerator in hopes that it would interact with the medication I had ingested and would get my task underway.

For a final measure, I placed a loaded shotgun in the passenger side seat of the car. Before heading to the car for what I planned on being the last time, I gathered my wedding album that was created for Megan and me, pictures of the boys, and the journal I had been keeping since the day Megan left.

I'd often write my thoughts down in the journal each morning as a way to cope, and this day, I wrote individual "goodbye notes" to my family. I placed all of this around me when I entered the car, which was already getting hazy inside with the exhaust gasses and vapors.

After sitting in there for approximately a half hour, my head began to spin, and I could tell that things were happening. I placed a call to Megan in hopes she would answer, but as expected, it went to voicemail. "Oh well, I had to try," I thought.

Another ten minutes went by, and I was getting very tingly in my legs, toes, and fingers. I never had a fear of what I was set out to do, rather, just a hope that it would hurry up and happen. I closed my eyes, only to reopen them to an incoming call from Megan.

She had seen that she missed my call and was calling me back. The signal was weak in the car, and apparently she was driving through an area of poor reception herself. She asked me what I needed, and I flat out told her what I was trying to accomplish. She apparently didn't catch much, if anything, I'd said before the call ended in a lost signal/disconnect.

Desperate to tell her and apologize one last time, I called her back. She answered and out of fear of losing the call again and wanting to desperately hear her voice, I instinctively moved out of the car and out of the garage to where the signal was stronger (at least on my end). This time I was able to tell her what I was doing to which I got a much deserved tongue-lashing as to how stupid I was for contemplating such a thing.

We talked to each other for almost ten minutes, during which time the fresh air was helping me regain a little stability in both my muscles and my common sense. After the call, I sat outside on the back porch and cried. I had hit what I thought was the bottom and couldn't believe it.

I credit the return call from Megan with the save that day. Had she not called me back and had written off my missed call as just another likely sob-fest, I would have succeeded with my attempt.

I went back to the garage, opened the door, and evacuated the toxins that had been generated. I cleaned the car from top to bottom that afternoon, telling myself that what I had been doing was not to be repeated.

I went to the store and picked up a large basket of wave petunias and took them to Megan's grandmother's home where Megan and Hunter were living at the time. She was a nice woman whom Megan thought a lot of, and vice versa.

She'd always been there for her in the past, and this was no different. I thanked her for being the port in the storm and taking good care of them when I couldn't. She was apprehensive about talking to me but understood to an extent where I was coming from.

As the conversation went on, I told her what actions I had taken earlier that day and that Megan's call was the one thing I credited with getting me through it. She told me I needed to get my shit straight, give Megan time, and let things happen as they are going to.

She couldn't speak for what Megan's intentions were but felt that if it were to work out, I needed to accomplish those things she mentioned. I thanked her for talking to me and headed home.

Ben's Insights

Many factors can cause a person to consider suicide. Medications can carry side effects of feeling suicidal, as can depression and anxiety. Suicidal thoughts are nothing to be discounted. If you find yourself feeling any feeling of hurting yourself or anyone else, seek help immediately.

Phone a friend, call the suicide prevention hotline, go to the hospital, or even just call 911. Thoughts and actions like those mentioned above are screams for help that are neither to be ignored nor taken lightly.

9—Bending Ears until They Break

After the attempt, I buckled down a bit and focused on the important things in my life, my kids. I spent weekends doing fun things when I had them, tackled a few home projects, and began to pursue job opportunities that would generate the income that I needed to not only take care of me, but prove to Megan that luck had changed back home in hopes she would return.

I awoke every day with a new confidence that everything would work out. I exercised, started hanging out with friends a little more, and seemed to be getting along better. I hung out with our old friends, who were still friends with Megan, and I was always asking how she was.

Even when she wasn't around, my thoughts were always on her. I wanted nothing more than to tell her about how my determination to better our lives was going and also to give an apology one more try. I used activities and my medication as coping mechanisms to thwart much of the depression and keep anxiety at bay, but every night when my head hit the pillow, the negative feelings settled in.

I hadn't brought myself to sleep in our bed since Megan had moved out two months prior and was getting less and less sleep each night. When I was really sad, I would go upstairs, lie on the bed, and hold her pillow, which still faintly smelled of her.

We still talked from time to time and saw each other, and our kids still hung out, which actually made things a little easier. I wanted her in my life any way I could get her and figured that in time perhaps I could show her I was working on making things better. She needed time to reset her finances to where it didn't stress her, time to digest everything that had happened, and time away from me. While I respected it, it wasn't a shared sentiment.

My heart and emotions would be top of the world when I was around her, and they sank when I wasn't. I became emotionally detached from other things that didn't involve her and lost myself in the process. Work was always the constant that I enjoyed, as it was a nine-hour distraction that I was good at. Coming home from work, I did homework with Ryan, made supper, and tried to enjoy evenings.

Many nights, I would call friends or receive calls from them to check in. If I told my story once, I told it a hundred times. After a month or so, I likely told the same people the same things more than once, and it never changed. I had the feeling that I'd bent everyone's ears on my situation, to which some understood and others didn't.

I began talking about my depression issues to a few people, but not many. Some thought it was just a case of the blues brought on by my current situation and blew it off. Others encouraged me to keep up my pills and coping mechanisms that I'd been doing and give it time.

I'd never been a patient person, and since life was in "crisis mode" for me, I wanted to make it stop and accomplish everything right then. With the urging of a friend, I looked into a therapist for help. I found a local office and made an appointment.

I had told the therapist on the phone the reason for my visit, and she assured me it wasn't uncommon. My appointment was spent with me confessing all of my emotions to her and crying the entire time. At the end of the visit, I left feeling a little better, knowing that I could add another possible coping mechanism to my arsenal of fighting my depression and anxiety.

I met with the therapist once every other week, and as the visits went by, fewer tears were shed and hope was slowly being restored in regard to my healing. I was starting to get a grasp on reality more but still wanted to fix what I'd done.

A coworker recommended a book to me (which I haven't read yet) titled *It's Called a Breakup Because It's Broken*. The title itself made sense to me, as I wanted more than anything to fix things. Hard as I had tried to convince Megan of any of this, I was met with rejection each time.

I just couldn't get my head around the fact that I was admitting my mistake, asking for forgiveness, yet not getting it. It boiled down to the fact that I had lost all of her trust by breaking the promises I'd made to be a responsible person. She felt she was fighting that battle herself, and it had taken its toll. Would time be the answer to her healing? I guess I'd have to wait and find out.

Ben's Insights

Therapy, which is highly recommended for coping with depression and anxiety disorders, is sometimes viewed as too invasive. Talking to strangers about something as sensitive as marital problems, financial woes, personal issues, and the like is more than some wish to talk about to someone they just met, no matter how highly qualified the therapist may be.

If this is the case, find a friend or family member whom you trust, and set aside time to open up and let it all out. Be ready to accept criticism and an opinion that might differ from that of your own.

Not everyone will understand, but many will try if the urgency is there. If the person can't relate or isn't as helpful as you had hoped, keep reaching out for someone who is. Help is out there.

Talking is coping, and coping is healing.

10—Hope for Change

The following weeks were filled with my trying to get back to a normal pace at work, which thankfully had gotten very busy. While it was stressful in its own right, working also gave me a chance to bury my personal emotions head down.

Once a day I found myself trolling the "Career Opportunities" section of our company site, reaching out to colleagues in the field for suggestions and even considering going back into the area that got me my start in the business. Change was fabled to be a good thing sometimes, so why not give it a try? Especially because it seemed nothing else was working.

I submitted a revised resume to our human resources department for a posting I found that caught my eye and scheduled an interview. It sounded promising, and I went home with a new confidence that something might finally shake loose and go my way.

Meanwhile, I had been networking with some friends with relationships with other companies and provided them also with my resume, but my heart was really set on staying with the company I was with. There is comfort in familiarity, something that I think affected all areas of my life.

As a volunteer firefighter, every other week we conducted training exercises to keep our skills sharp. There was a business that had recently been remodeled in our town, so we conducted what was called a fire pre-plan, consisting of a walkthrough of the building during which we located important things like electrical breaker boxes, locations of fire extinguishers, sprinkler system checks, etc.

The owner of the business was an old acquaintance of mine, and he and I struck up a conversation about work. The subject of making a change came about, and he suggested we meet in a few days to discuss an opportunity he might have for me. Of course, I was immediately excited.

The location was literally two blocks from my home, the business was financially strong, and it was an industry that I was familiar with, so there would be very little training needed before I was up and running.

Things sounded promising on the job fronts, and, during this timeframe, Megan and I started keeping in touch more. I was able to see her and her son more, which was not only good for me, but for the boys too. They got to be together, which offset their sadness.

Every day I got more and more hopeful for a chance that the breakup and impending divorce might all be undone with her seeing that I had promising things on the horizon with a better paying job.

Depression was always a factor though. I still wasn't getting near the sleep I needed to be getting, I was losing weight like crazy because of a lack of appetite, and my drinking seemed to be the only way I was getting the calories I needed anymore. Through all of this though, I managed to keep my children in the forefront of my priorities.

With my sons, I always made sure that homework was done, that we spent quality time together, and that they knew they were loved. Work and the kids were the only constants I had, and I took great care to ensure that those stayed intact.

Just as I thought things were better, I received the final divorce papers in the mail. There it was, in five cruel pages of black and white, the end of something I valued so much. It was plain and simple, not hard to decipher, but the hardest words to swallow were the reasons for the filing: "irreconcilable differences."

That one went straight to my soul. This is about the time that I knew that no matter what I was doing, it was not working. There was no stopping either this or my descent into the rabbit hole of depression.

There weren't enough medications, therapists, miles to jog, or distractions that would counter the effects that I was personally feeling, so I began to turn my thoughts to a more serious attempt at suicide.

Ben's Insights

No mention or thought of suicide should ever be taken lightly. Some of the warning signs that are commonly found to be linked to suicide are talking about life not being worth living, expressions of feelings of being helpless or worthless, withdrawing from family, friends, or usual activities, and experiencing a change in personality, such as becoming more down and withdrawn or more irritable and explosive.

If you or a loved one suffers from depression or anxiety and these behaviors are witnessed or experienced, seek assistance as soon as possible.

11—Goodbye Is All We've Got Left to Say

I held out hope that the word about the new job would arrive soon so that the possibility of money could fill the void, again a kind of "Band-Aid" of sorts to cover the pain of my loss. After all, something had to go right, right? I'd surely suffered enough loss in the previous 15 months. I prayed for mercy, I asked for a change of luck, I swore to do whatever was needed to make it stop.

One night, just to say I tried absolutely everything, I spoke aloud and offered my soul in exchange for the pain to stop and the sun to once again come out in my life. Nobody replied or took me up on the offer so that proved to me I was truly alone.

After five months of waiting on something to shake loose on the career front, my marriage collapsing, and my stress level higher than I could take, I decided what I was going to do if I was going to do it.

I went to my mother's house one morning to pick up my son who'd spent the night there the evening before. She lived alone after my parent's divorce, and she acquired a .38mm revolver shortly after my dad moved out. With her home being located in a very rural area, it gave her and us peace of mind knowing that she was armed if needed.

The seller of the gun even threw in bullets for it, including one hollow-point. Hollow-point bullets are designed to absolutely shred whatever they hit as their design makes them mushroom out once they impact, leaving more of a hole exiting than when they entered.

I made my way back to my mother's room, knowing where she kept it, and snuck it into my pocket. It was already loaded, so I didn't bother grabbing a box of ammunition. Once home, I placed the gun high and away from where the kids would find it, and went about my day.

That evening, I recall giving myself a deadline to accomplish a list of goals. My patience had run its course regarding the wait for everything I wanted. It seemed clear to me that nothing was going to work out as it should, no matter how hard I tried.

My medication might as well have been Skittles, my drinking was once again getting bad, and my other symptoms of depression were out of control as well.

That week, I made a pretty conscious attempt to visit family, make contact with friends, spend the time I could with my kids, and mentally satisfy my need to say goodbye.

I remember the last person I said goodbye to was my friend Joel, next door. He was the last person I saw that day, and I remember the day well.

My plan was to accomplish this on a weekend that I didn't have my kids. I would be completely alone when this was to take place, but after that ... well, whoever found me would have an unfortunate surprise.

I told NOBODY of my intentions, as I didn't want to place that burden on anyone, and, truthfully, at that point, I don't think a single person could have talked me out of it. I was no longer myself. I had fully succumbed to the hopelessness, worthlessness, despair, and misery of my sickness.

It was a beautiful, sunny Saturday in July. The 18th to be exact. I mowed the yard that morning, washed the car, walked my dogs, drank my coffee outside, and cleaned up the house. After all, I didn't want to leave it any messier than I would likely get it later.

Shortly after lunch, I walked over to my friend Joel's house and stopped in for a quick visit. They had plans that afternoon, so I didn't stick around long. I remember the feeling of almost telling him what I was thinking, but I didn't as I walked out the door for what I knew would be the last time.

When I look back on that afternoon, I almost get chills because it was like, for a fleeting moment, the old me that had common sense tried to come back up to the surface but was beaten back down by the emotional demons that had taken up residence. I made the walk back home and began to prepare.

I walked in the door, remembering that I was calm and confident about what I had been planning to do. I sat down on the couch and watched television for a little bit just to escape reality one last time.

I placed a call to Megan, but it once again went to her voicemail. After all, she was the reason that my previous attempt was avoided, and down deep—I was letting fate decide if it would happen again.

I told myself if she called me back before the end of the show I was watching, I wouldn't go through with it. As it turned out, no call came, so I went to the kitchen and retrieved the gun and the bullet.

I sat back down on the couch and just looked at the bullet that I intended to use. It was in all essence the pill that I would take to end it all. The proverbial pill to end the pain. I placed the bullet into the chamber and spun it.

I recall looking down the barrel to see if it landed on it, but it didn't. I respun it once more, this time not looking, and pulled the trigger.

What happened next is something I will never forget.

I remember two things quite vividly—the sound of the shot as it went off under my chin and the feeling that I'd just been hit point-blank in the face with a baseball bat. The force of the shot whipped my head straight up, and I immediately thought, "Holy shit."

The ringing in my ears was absolutely deafening, and I rose from the couch to stand but fell back down. Immediately, I realized a few things. First, I realized I had actually gone through with it, something that I wasn't sure I'd have the ability to do. Secondly, I realized that I was still alive but had no idea as to what shape I was in.

As I had only placed one bullet into the gun, I realized I would have to go get another one and try again, but I was in no shape to make it back to the kitchen at the moment. I remember trying once again to stand, but couldn't.

I instead crawled weakly towards the kitchen and then just lay on the floor. I was bleeding profusely from my mouth, chin, and nose, losing a pretty good amount of blood. I grabbed a nearby pillow to rest my head on because, of course, my head hurt. I remember thinking that if I could just get my body to cooperate and make the walk back to Joel's house, I might be able to get help. After all, I was still alive, conscious, but admittedly—fading fast.

The last effort to stand once again failed, and I remember just hoping that I'd pass out. If I passed out, I felt I could go in my sleep from the loss of blood and the trauma. Surely my body would just shut down as the bleeding continued.

I had one last thought on my mind, so I grabbed my phone. I once again called Megan, but this time to say goodbye. Voicemail was received once again, and apparently I left a message, then hung up, and called 911. I got the operator. I tried to tell her what happened and was asking her to call Megan to say my goodbye for me.

The dispatcher couldn't understand me very well due to the damage of the gunshot. The impact of the bullet shattered my jaw in three places, did significant damage to my tongue, went through the roof of my mouth and bounced around in the frontal area of skull and sinuses. Hollow-point bullets are advertised for the exceptional damage they do, and this one was no different.

The dispatcher finally made out what I was saying, and, before I knew it, she was dispatching help. My fire pager was in the kitchen, and, within seconds, I heard my address and situation being transmitted to my department and our local rescue team.

She said she would try to reach Megan, and then I hung up.

Within a few minutes, I heard my name being called as the county sheriff entered my home. He had been our town cop previously and was a good friend of ours. I couldn't see at this point, as I was drifting in and out of consciousness.

Later, I learned that the damage to my frontal area detached the retina in my left eye, shattering the socket of that eye as well. The right eye was functioning, but was black and blue and swelling fast.

He asked me questions that I tried to answer, but my words were muffled due to the blood I was spitting out and my mouth being in pieces. Within another few minutes, several members of our first responder team showed up and began treating me. I passed out several times, and, when I came to, I remember hearing the roar of the helicopter as they loaded me on the stretcher towards the air care unit.

In the past, whenever I saw or heard an air care helicopter flying overhead, I would make the comment, "Someone's having a bad day." Never did I imagine before that I would be one of those passengers, but it was happening.

The last words I heard were from my friend, Kyle Negangard, a fellow firefighter and long time friend, who was cursing at me for doing this and also telling me that he was going to administer something to put me out. After that, I recall nothing else of that afternoon.

Ben's Insights

While not everyone who battles depression considers suicide, it is quite common. In fact, depression is the single greatest risk factor for suicide.

Two-thirds of all suicides are linked to depression directly. A recent study has shown that 15 percent of people who are depressed commit suicide as a result of it. It is worth noting also that these numbers are on the rise in both completed and attempted suicides. Girls have a higher percentage of attempts while boys have a higher completion rate.

The top risk factors for suicide have been found to be having a family history of suicide, suffering from disorders that affect emotions and behavior, experiencing stressful life events, being rejected or abandoned by a specific person (husband, wife, loved one, etc), drugs and alcohol, and being impulsive.

12—Dismantle. Repair

Whatever drug Kyle gave me did the job, as I don't recall one second of my $40,000 plus helicopter ride from my home to UC Hospital in Cincinnati, Ohio. I wish I did though, as riding in a helicopter was always on my bucket list of things to do before I died. Little did I know that I almost accomplished both in the same day...

After speaking with family, friends, and staff about my first couple of days in the hospital, I came to the realization that it's best I didn't recall much. From their accounts, here are the details I gathered:

I was brought in and treatment was administered by a full staff of ER surgeons: plastics, trauma, general surgeons, and ophthalmologists. When I first arrived, they said both of my eyes were black and blue and badly swollen. Under my chin, a grown man could place four fingers into the hole made by the entry of the bullet.

My tongue had a hole clean through it, and they had to work very hard on getting enough muscle together to stitch it closed. The roof of my mouth had an opening the size of a half dollar, and the sinus cavities of my frontal skull were shattered, along with the orbital socket of my left eye.

The bullet came to rest between my left eye and my nasal passage. It was later discovered that the bullet came within a hair or two of entering my brain, which would have been a whole different story.

After the team stabilized my condition, I was placed in the ICU, where apparently I was touch and go. Defibrillators were used twice, and the nurses later told me that the staff honestly didn't think I would make it past the second day.

My parents were attending a German festival that day, so they were out of contact until late that evening. The medical staff had to wait to get consent to treat me further, and, after several failed attempts, Kyle (the same friend and firefighter who came to my rescue) got in touch with Megan.

He told her of my situation and said it might come down to her having to consent to my care. As she was preparing to do this, my parents were reached, gave the okay, and treatment was underway.

I apparently had several folks that came up that evening and stayed until the early hours of the morning until medical staff declared that I was stable enough for them to go home and rest. That evening, I slept.

The next day, I came to. Not knowing where I was, exactly how long I'd been there, or what condition I was in was a scary thing. I couldn't talk at all, and my only form of communication with anyone was by spelling/writing letters on the bed sheet or my chest with my fingers.

Many times questions were simply yes or no, or ones that could be answered with thumbs up or down. Pain was always calculated on a scale of 1 to 10, and, thankfully, I didn't have to use both hands to relay this information too many times.

They did a great job in managing this for me. I slept quite a bit, and this is where the dreams started.

During the entire course of my hospital stay, which lasted almost five whole weeks, I had the most vivid and convincing dreams that I've ever had. I remember almost every one of them, too.

Some were very relaxing, some were scary. Still, they were always fun to look forward to, and, over time, it became hard to determine if they were real or not.

I'm not sure what prompted any of them because, with my vision being bad, I didn't watch television and in a hospital it's not like you have much stimulation from the outside world about which to dream. My imagination was left to its own devices, which was scary and fun at the same time.

Over the next few days, I was visited by friends and family, some of whom I'd not seen or heard from in a long time. It was nice to visit with them but unfortunate due to the circumstances.

One of my best friends, Paul, came up just about every night. He and I would often visit for a couple of hours at a time. We talked about everything from old cars, happenings going on back home, the Cincinnati Reds and Bengals, as well as our favorite shared topic—old Pontiacs.

Paul and I have been friends for about 20 years and have shared many stories and even cars! One particular evening, Paul brought me a license plate. Not just any license plate, but one that was on the front of one of the old cars I had owned a few years prior.

It adorned the front end of a 1964 Pontiac Tempest, and it simply said, "BOCEPHUS." The car had previously been owned by an old man who was apparently a Hank, Jr. fan, so we found it humorous and decided to nickname the car the same name.

I asked Paul how he'd gotten the plate back, as it was on the car when I sold it. He informed me that he had gotten the car back and was giving it to me to work on once I got myself out of the hospital.

He said it was fitting that it was the last old Pontiac I'd ever owned, and it needed just as much repair as I did. He envisioned me helping it, and it doing the same for me. From that evening on, I had been given another reason to get myself better and back to life. In the days to come, the license plate became quite the topic of conversation with the staff and visitors alike.

Once I was stable, the real work began. Approximately three days after my admission, surgery was performed to reconstruct the bones in my face and also to retrieve the bullet fragments. A bone graft was required (which really does hurt), and the harvested material was used to repair above and below my eye socket as well as the cheekbone area on my left side. The surgery itself was quite extensive and indicative of those to come.

The next surgery I had was to repair my jaw, which involved grafting bone once again from my hip and repairing the three areas that were broken. Miraculously, I didn't lose one single tooth to the injury; however, it completely rearranged my upper and lower mandibles, causing serious misalignment of my teeth.

This is something that the doctors said would have to wait at least six months before repairing as to give the bones time to mend. Once the repair was made, they wired my jaw shut, and I was to remain that way for six weeks.

I was already getting my "food" and medicines through what's known as a "G-tube" into my stomach, and the doctors said it would likely be three to four months before I could consider solid foods again. I remember the sinking feeling that I might miss Thanksgiving dinner, which was always my favorite holiday.

The last surgery during my stay was to correct the damage done to my left eye itself. The retina had detached, and I had a steady bleed that was filling the eye. Thankfully my right eye sustained very minor damage and was able to heal on its own. I was taken for surgery and very nervous about it. I'd had detached retina surgery before on both eyes, but this surgery was due to a trauma.

I wasn't sure to what degree the damage was, and neither were the doctors that were going to perform the surgery. Hearing "We'll know more once we get in there" doesn't always calm your nerves. Thankfully it went off fine, but there was still damage that would need to be addressed after the healing process.

Every time I looked in the mirror at my reflection, I had new evidence of what I'd gone through looking right back at me. I guess the old saying that "Bigger scars make better stories" was going to be the case here. I definitely was looking at my fair share of them.

Everyday it seemed I was being told how surprisingly quickly I was healing and how much ahead of plan I was in regards to my condition. I had apparently been recovering quite quickly and soon earned the nickname "Wolverine," after the Marvel Comics character who had the ability to heal quickly from wounds and damage.

It was kind of an inspiration for me, as I didn't want to be in that hospital any longer than I had to be. Little did I know that healing the body was only part of the battle, and that real battle was getting ready to start.

I made it a point to get out of bed each day and walk the halls, move around and try to stay as active outside of the bed as I could. I was only allowed to stay on my floor, so the halls and I became very acquainted over the weeks to come. I began recognizing faces and, in some cases, voices (since my vision wasn't up to par yet). I became good friends with much of the nursing staff, who continued to root on my progress.

One particular nurse, whose name was Kirk, was super. He was apparently there the night they'd brought me in and was likely close to my age. As time went on, he and I became good friends. Many nights he would listen as I confided to him about what led me to do what I did, and he did his best to keep my spirits up.

I enjoyed having someone there who was neutral in everything, to hear my story and not be judgmental in anything. That was absolutely refreshing to be honest.

Over the course of my stay, I had plenty of visits from family and friends. It was nice to look forward to the company, but at the same time, it was nice to have time to reflect on everything that led me to where I was at the moment—an uncomfortable hospital bed with critical injuries and surgeries to come, a long road to recovery, and an uncertain future ahead of me.

Not exactly where a man who just hit what is considered to be a milestone age of 40 ever thought he'd be. I envisioned myself having a great year celebrating, and, instead, I was looking at spending at least a year recuperating.

From time to time, the psychological staff members would stop in to ask me how I was doing and if I had thoughts of hurting myself or others that day, in attempt to get an overall idea of how my mental status was. To hear them ask this was a bit degrading actually, as I didn't see myself as still a risk at all.

I felt okay, just a bit embarrassed and regretful that I did it. I had no desires to go through that again, or put anyone else through it. By telling them that, I felt I was convincing myself. I was, wasn't I?

Truthfully, at first when I recovered and learned what I had been through, I was upset. Upset that I didn't succeed. Upset that I did nothing but make my already difficult and miserable life even MORE miserable and difficult. Not only did I have to keep coping with the stress that I had before, I had to burden myself and others with even more.

Why couldn't that bullet have just done more damage? Why did I have to live? Why didn't it work? Why why why?

I had a period of a week where this is all I asked myself. Every day, I put on a happy face and learned how much progress I had made. Learned how I would likely be released to the next phase of my treatment in a few weeks. A few weeks. Wow. Days felt like weeks, weeks like months, and my stay seemed endless.

I had lost track of the days of the week—and didn't give a shit. They all meant the same—another day of waking up, wishing I was either healed completely and over it all, or wishing I would've just died.

It was becoming clearer that my depression didn't go away with the pulling of the trigger or the removal of the bullet. The surgeons didn't find "the twins" in my head and remove them too when they were in there retrieving the bullet fragments. No, that would be too easy.

Unfortunately, I was still keeping company with the twins there in the hospital despite the cocktail of medications I was on. They had full access to my waking hours and my sleeping hours since nothing was there as a coping mechanism to keep them at bay.

My dreams were their playing field. Every night, I had horrible dreams that ranged from seeing Megan with another man, having several of my deceased relatives coming to visit me, and even my kids perishing in an ambulance fire. Yeah—dreams can be nightmares. I can tell you all about that.

One afternoon, I received a visit from a couple of my coworkers who told me they had a present for me. Apparently, fellow workers pooled some funds together and purchased a Kindle Fire tablet for me. They figured a hospital bed was a boring place to be, so something like this would be just what I needed.

It turned out to be true! I had been asking about my iPad, but according to my family, the police officers had taken it along with my cell phone when they came to the scene. The Kindle allowed me to watch Netflix, listen to Pandora radio, and surf the Internet. Life outside the room was just a keystroke away. This was a wonderful present and very appreciated.

Over the next couple days, I actually began thinking about things again in my life. My thoughts once again went back to what I personally felt was wrong in my life for me—my relationship with Megan, my role as a father to my kids, and what I could be doing to approach a better career path at work.

My mind went from the slow pace of sitting and watching the clock, to a furious speed where I envisioned actually making something good come of all of it. I mentally dismantled my life and rebuilt it in several different scenarios, all coming to an ending where I could possibly be happy and put the nightmares of the past behind me.

I just needed to find an equation that I thought would work. Surely, I was capable of doing this. At least I thought I was. I just needed to put some pieces in the right order or leave some of them out.

One evening during Kirk's rotation, I asked him just how long I'd been there. I'd not seen a calendar, which made sense as what I had nothing to look forward to besides an upcoming surgery, right? I learned that I'd been in there for over four weeks.

To this point, I'd really not given it much deep thought, as I'd been back in the rabbit hole with depression again. But the days prior to my asking, I had been wrenching in my mind all of the ideas I needed to accomplish for a complete overhaul of my life.

This question then had me wondering another one—*what all had changed in almost a month that I'd been in the hospital?* I had grown an impressive beard, that much I knew, but in all seriousness—*what all was going on?*

I'd gotten some reports from my parents and friends, but they seemed to be all screened answers as to not upset me in regards to what was happening in the real world. I asked several times how my dogs were, the house was, how my sons were and the like, and felt I was missing some information.

Finally, one afternoon, I asked my Dad and his wife Lori about what was going on. They sat down and broke the news to me that shortly after I was admitted to the hospital, they and a large group of friends went to my house and moved me out completely. Over the course of one afternoon, I went from having a home I was dreaming of returning to once I got out of the hospital, to not having a home at all.

I was told that I'd been relocated to my mother's home, and all of my belongings were being held either in her basement, in our pole barn, or in a paid storage facility. My life as I knew it was once again changed forever.

They stated the reason being that since the home was empty, they didn't want people coming and potentially having things disappear. Also, there was no clear-cut indication as to how long my stay in the hospital was going to be (and apparently when this was first decided, I was still in the ICU, where they weren't even sure I was going to make it through a couple of days).

There was no way to know if I was going to be gone from there a week, month, or a year, so they made the decision to move me out. The home was being purchased via land contract, so they contacted the owner and worked it out to where I was released from the agreement.

With an afternoon's worth of work and the stroke of a pen, I was homeless, and all of the plans I had made in my head to rebuild my life suddenly had another "X factor" to work around. At first, I understood completely and saw their perspective. But as time went on, I felt more and more robbed of everything.

My dreams and goals I had been working on, my plans to go home after I accomplished getting out of the hospital, the equity I had built over the years of being there, and, lastly, my privacy—were gone. Imagining people I both know and don't know, walking through my home putting my things in boxes and bags, touching my memories and denying me of the ability to say goodbye to that place set in, and I was filled with sadness once again.

Stress and depression ... you win this round again.

Ben's Insights

According to Dr. Bizhan Aarabi, director of neurotrauma at the Maryland Shock Trauma Center, 20,000 people in the United States die each year from gunshot wounds to the head. The survival rate is about 5 percent, with only 3 percent achieving a good quality of life afterward.

My depression and anxiety brought me to this event in my life, and I knew that if I was going to live through it, it would be a hard road ahead. "If it is to be, it's up to me" was my thought. Developing the goals for healing and the determination to get better and make something more of my life as well as vowing never to go down that path again were all goals that I set for myself.

It's not a path that many can do alone, and I was no different. Through a network of therapists, friends, family, and medical staff, each day became better than the previous one.

Still, depression and anxiety were a mere thought or mood away. Treatment for these illnesses have to be integral with the rest of the injuries, as they are just as damaging. Never assume that treatment of one cures all.

13—“Hello.” “Hey.”

A few days later, while working on the Kindle, I entertained the thought of sending an email to Megan just to say hello. I had learned that my parents didn’t want her there at the hospital due to the fact that they believed my suicide attempt was solely due to her.

They and others feared that seeing her might do me more harm than good. Little did they know that I was feeling the loss of her once again. Granted, many would view this as the mourning process and the natural process one would go through after a divorce or the loss of a loved one.

To me, she was not just the love of my life, but my best friend even through all the ugliness of the divorce. I may never have her back as my wife, but I surely didn’t want to lose her as my friend. That would be a little more loss than I was comfortable in taking.

I kept my thoughts private and began wondering what to say. After all, it had been almost an entire month since the incident. *What if she was with someone? What if she had moved and was no longer around? What if something bad happened? Heck—what if she didn't want to hear from me?*

My previously mentioned dreams that I'd had while in the hospital stirred up emotions that I felt I needed to resolve, so I made the decision to draft a letter. I bet I started and stopped that email five dozen times, only to finally hit the "send" button. I didn't have the ability to send her a text or make a phone call, so I sent it to her work email. To my absolute surprise, I got a reply shortly after.

I sat there completely surprised and half scared to death to even open it. Would it be a warm reception to my email or a hate-filled rant about what I'd done? With a deep breath and nervous hand, I clicked open the email.

To my amazement, she seemed surprised and somewhat happy to hear from me. She asked how I was doing, and, before long, we were emailing back and forth consistently. It became something I looked forward to each and every day, and kind of made all of the experience easier to talk about.

We discussed all of the surgeries, the treatments, and the incident itself. She seemed interested in hearing it all, which helped me too, as I hadn't really talked to anyone at that point in great detail about things (with the exception of Kirk, who was like my evening bartender). To say it was uplifting to have contact with her again is an understatement.

I'd be lying to say that I didn't want more to come of it, but I knew better. I made the comment once to her about how I missed her, and she said that she felt comfortable emailing me but had no desire to see me as there had been too much going on and too many things had transpired for her to ever want to see me again.

She was fine being email friends only. Hey, at this point, I was more than happy to take it. I missed talking to her and hearing about her life as well as her son, Hunter. I felt like I'd been in a coma for years when I heard about all the things that I'd been missing out on in the five weeks I'd been in there.

But instead of bringing me down, it had a very different effect on me. The newfound "friendship" actually inspired me to blow the dust off my goals, work harder on my therapy, and actually improved my attitude overall. I recall the next day after that first email reply, the lead doctor of my trauma team, which made morning rounds regularly, made the comment that he saw an actual improvement in how I was doing.

That same day, the psychology team also visited and made the same observation. It seemed the emails were the motivation I needed. Something as simple as communication with Megan once again put wind in my sails, filling me with a sense of determination to get better and get the hell back to life.

I wasn't expecting anything other than that daily communication, which was more than fine with me, but just having that piece of my puzzle back was something that seemed so familiar in what had recently become a scattered mess of my life. I viewed my emails as an avenue to tell someone about all of the things I had been dealing with before, during, and after the incident—the surgeries and the emotions I had been experiencing—it was relieving!

During our conversations, I learned truths about many things I hadn't previously known, and some of them angered me while others came as no surprise. There was lots of chatter going on back home about what I'd done, and rumors and stories of all kinds were circulating. I expected this, because I don't believe there was one person who had any idea of my plans that day. It angered me to hear that many people were holding Megan responsible for what I did, and not taking into account all of the other things I had going on to deal with. She resented this, and I agreed with her. We had many colorful email chats about the things that had transpired since the accident, and it was just as crazy sounding and emotional as it was before. Still, I was happy just to talk to her again and tried to keep things on an even keel.

I simply concentrated on getting better more and more every day, and leaving the hospital bed. Besides the communication with Megan and Hunter, I was craving my own kids, who were not brought up to see me while I was in the hospital out of fear it might traumatize them.

I hated the thought of going any longer than I had to before I could see them, but I knew it was the right call. We were able to use Facetime once, and it was so nice to see and hear them that way. It was another motivator to get my spirits and therapy moving in the right direction.

While it was an easy task in convincing myself that my happiness and emotions were improving,

proving it to the psychological staff at the hospital was another matter. Once my physical treatment and repairs had been done, I was to be moved to a completely different hospital for the mental rebuilding phase of my treatment.

This would prove to be a very trying experience, one I wasn't quite sure about, but I knew that it was to be the last step in my path to being released and back on the road of my life, so I was eager to take the next step, with dedication in my mind towards the goals I had set, as well as the desire to get the heck out of there.

Nothing in this world can take the place of persistence. Talent will not: nothing is more common than unsuccessful men with talent. Genius will not: unrewarded genius is almost a proverb. Education will not: the world is full of educated derelicts. Persistence and determination alone are omnipotent.

—Calvin Coolidge

Ben's Insights

When receiving treatment for depression, it's important to be absolutely honest in regards to what's working and what's not, if you're truly seeing change inside and if so, is it good or bad.

Therapy, as mentioned earlier, can often feel invasive, but it's often necessary when other avenues or attempts aren't fully working. The power of connecting with someone can be most effective. Some reach for this option first, others wait until things get very hard. It's up to the individual to determine the effectiveness of any treatment, but with the help of others it can be easier.

14—Xanadu

As my physical treatment and recovery reached the point where I was ready for discharge, my next stop was to move to a facility where I could be treated for the mental part of my journey. Because of the nature, reason, and extreme result of my injury, mental therapy was necessary before I could officially be released and leave the care of the physicians.

No sweat, right? I was feeling better as of late, the pains and ordeal I had been through the past month surely weren't anything I wanted to ever repeat, and the sad faces and fears of my family and friends were something I didn't want to have to see again anytime soon either.

I was to move to a different hospital across town, where they were set up to treat patients for mental disorders. I'd heard stories about the building itself, which was an older eight-story hospital that now only operated on three floors.

The original hospital went out of business several years previously and now was being partially leased out by another hospital for outpatient treatment.

This left most of the building empty, and stories of haunted floors and old surgical and trauma wings with resident ghosts were often told to me by the nursing staff, which sure made me look forward to my upcoming visit even more!

I was told the average stay for patients like me was approximately three to five days, which, after the stay I had just gone through recovering from my trauma, would likely be a breeze.

I made the move to the new place on Friday and began my treatment almost immediately. The staff seemed friendly, and the residents were, well, residents for a reason. My case was a bit unique there. I was the only one that was being treated for depression while others were there for more severe mental illness like Alzheimer's and dementia.

I was definitely in unique company, that's for sure! The staff and doctors urged participation in both group and individual sessions, arguing that it was necessary to show progress in order to prove readiness for discharge. With that being my clear intention, I dove right in.

The counselors on the floor, all aware of my reason for being there, were sympathetic to my situation. I was not given special treatment by any means, but they did handle me a little differently regarding the course of my treatments and therapies.

While group sessions typically consisted of "craft hour" and discussion time, the individual / one-on-one session was more personalized. I usually met with the primary psychiatrist and two of their fellows or residents. We would discuss the typical things, like feelings of depression, suicide, and my personal progress.

It was during this time that I was quizzed hard about what led me to making the decisions that got me to that place. I shared every reason I had, but apparently the therapy team had it in their heads that I was holding back and not placing the cause on the right things.

I had adopted an honesty-was-the best-policy type approach during the course of all of this but was really feeling like they were not going to believe me. Instead of simply agreeing with them and just telling them what they wanted to hear, I became more determined and vocal that they were wrong and they needed to believe what I was saying.

They insisted that my reason for the attempt was due to the breakdown of my marriage and to no other factor. While I will admit that it was a factor, it certainly was not the sole factor, but they couldn't understand.

I went into detail about how important work was in my life, my always present desire to become the best at what I did and never stop climbing the ladder of success pertaining to it, and how it was something I took pride in. The medical expert that was assigned to me actually argued with me, stating that work shouldn't play that big of a role in my life and that a job was just a job.

This was something that I took great offense to, and I let him know it. Boy, was that a mistake. I was told that my anger regarding this issue led him to believe that I had deeper issues that needed resolving.

I was reminded at that time that the normal stay for patients like me was three to five days, but if they felt that I needed more time, they would place me under what's known as "probate" where I would be admitted under a type of court order and the physician could keep me there until a time to be decided by them only. He was leaning towards this option but wanted to bring in my family to discuss my progress further before he ultimately made the decision.

My heart sank, and I felt imprisoned once again. I could no longer see the light at the end of the tunnel, and I felt hopelessness creeping in all over again. *God, how did I get to this point in my life? Granted I had made bad decisions, but what person hasn't at one point in their life? Sure, I had a great streak of bad luck happening in my life, but at what point was enough enough?* I kept thinking. I was truly reaching my breaking point. I remember lying in bed, crying, and asking the heavens to please see that I was waving the white flag. I'd surrendered.

I didn't think there was a single additional negative thing that I could take anymore. I went to bed that night feeling completely lost. At this point, I had been there four days, one day longer than I needed to in my mind, but one day shy of the max they needed to keep me unless I was going to be admitted under probate. The next day was absolutely critical, the day that my family was to come in for the consult with the therapy staff and myself present.

The concern that everyone had was that I was going to get out of the hospital, get home, fall back into the groove of depression, and make an attempt to finish what I started. While I can see their point, nobody seemed to see my new point of view that I had opened my eyes to in the hospital.

I shared with many the new outlook I had and the goals that I had determined for myself, but I kept a few to myself knowing that they might be viewed negatively with all that had gone on. While they all seemed to listen to me, I looked around the room at that meeting and saw faces of doubt.

Understandable, because nobody in that room ever wanted to be put in that situation ever again, but at the same time, I didn't either. While I'd readied myself for what I envisioned as a fight for my life and sanity, it turned out somewhat docile. There were times of tension, but in the end, they all agreed that me getting back to work and on with my life, moving forward with the goals I had set, would be just as effective of a therapy session as what they in the hospital could ever provide.

I agreed to participate in therapy sessions once released and would also provide follow-ups to the staff in regards to my progress. After much consideration, the staff ultimately decided to release me and not to probate me any further. I couldn't believe it—I was finally going home!

I spent that evening saying thank you to God and the heavens above, and promising to follow up and make good on the changes in my life that I promised I would do. I gladly packed my clothes and walked the halls that evening with a smile on my face. I don't recall any feelings of depression, just happy anxiety, knowing that the next morning I would be loading up in the car and never looking back.

Ben's Insights

Being placed in the institute was very depressing in its own right but was required by those deciding my treatment. I first met the idea with my feet in the sand, but with the help of a counselor there, I realized that my path to better mental health was going to be a daily battle, not just a state of mind depending on what side of the bed I woke up on. The trained staff there realize that facilities like that are often the extreme "end of the line" options for those with severe depression ... far more severe than mine, believe it or not. They are skilled healers that treat each case individually and work hard to get to the root of the problem and help.

Being there for that week absolutely made me realize that my course of happiness was up to me and that I needed to be bigger than whatever obstacle or problem was in front of me. I practice this every day.

15—Dark Is a Place; Light Is the Way

Walking out of the secured door on the floor of the mental unit, I felt much like an inmate who'd finally been pardoned and was leaving the iron bars of the prison yard for the first time. I heard the *click* of the latch behind me as I hit the elevator button to take me to the lobby.

As I stepped outside to the curb and felt the fresh air hit my cheeks and fill my lungs, I had a tear trickle down my cheek. The warm breeze was certainly welcome from the constantly frigid temperatures that are associated with the hospital rooms that I'd been a resident of for the past six weeks. I couldn't believe it. I was going home.

As my mom pulled around the corner and up to the curb, I also realized that while I was ready to go home, I wasn't necessarily ready to jump back into everything completely just yet. I had several follow-up appointments scheduled for everything from my eyes to my jaw and trauma repairs.

I was also looking at physical therapy for my tongue and mouth, and had at least one or two more surgeries coming up to remove the metal from my mouth and finally close the hole that I'd created in the roof of my mouth. These were all things that would take place in the next few weeks or months, and, of course, I had the visits scheduled with my psychiatrist as well.

I wasn't allowed to return to work or do anything too normal for several weeks, but I was going to need the time to rest and heal. Since my home had basically been surrendered, I was released to the care of my mom, who had set me up in my old room at her house.

I wasn't sure just what to expect there since the whole time prior to learning this, I was looking forward to going "home." I arrived and found a nice setup, however, and was appreciative of the gesture. Still, it wasn't the same. I was set up there, as it was just my Mom and her two cocker spaniels living there.

My Mom was also one of the troopers who came up just about every day, and was also excited to see my return home. Many nights we would sit and talk about all of the pain I was going through, and she was a good listener for this.

She volunteered to let me stay there and to provide the care I was going to need for the following weeks. While this was going to be a change for me to go through, it was also going to be one for her as well. It had been a long time since she'd had one of her kids back home.

Speaking of kids, I did get a welcome surprise in the form of my own boys, Ryan and Evan. Their mother brought them over, and we had a nice visit. They asked questions ranging from "Did it hurt?" to "Can we see what they did?" Surprisingly, they weren't scared of my swollen and scarred appearance. Instead, they had made drawings and get-well cards for me, and had plenty of hugs to share. It made my first afternoon home a very nice one.

They were aware of what I had done but were unaware as to why. There are some things that little kids just don't need to know, and there was no reason to ask them to deal with this very adult issue. They were just happy to see me alive and doing well.

That evening, my friend Paul, that to this point was basically the one person who came and saw me more than anyone, sent me a text, asking if I was in the mood to get out of the house for a while. *Of course!* The plan was to just have a low-key evening, seeing some friends and checking out some of the old cars that I'd been missing out on.

He came and picked me up, and we had a good night catching up with folks who were also very happy to see me, and it was a great way to have a homecoming. I also had the chance to see Bocephus once again, the 1964 Tempest that was awaiting my repairs. It looked a little changed from the last time I'd seen it, but it was still the same shade of green it had been previously. I tapped it on the hood and told the car that we'd get better together.

In the weeks that followed, I attended several follow-ups, therapy sessions, and evenings out and about. Progress towards getting life back to normal was finally taking shape, and while it wasn't happening quite as quickly as I'd have liked it to, it was happening nonetheless. I had several friends who sent me texts, emails, and instant messages through Facebook and the like, wishing me luck and congratulating me on my recovery.

It was a nice feeling having cheerleaders in my corner, and it made me quite determined to keep moving forward. Still, I wasn't completely settled in emotionally because, while I was out of the hospital, I still wasn't home.

There's something scary and intimidating about change. I was happy to be out and recovering, but I still felt like there were many things in my life that weren't resolved. I had feelings of sadness knowing that I would never be returning to my life as I once knew it (before the depression took hold) because so many things had changed.

I tried everyday to relate to the old me, but it became harder than I thought it would be. My friends were still my friends, but I couldn't help but notice they all saw me differently whether it was based on my looks or just the reality of what I'd done. Like it or not, nothing was going to be the same.

With my home having been surrendered, I found myself at a crossroads. *Do I move back to the same area I was before? Do I find a place closer to work (although many of the areas around here are places I don't really care to live) or do I pull stakes and start afresh somewhere far away but not* too *far?*

These are decisions that I will make as I can.

Reacclimating to life is something that I am learning to do each day. Thankfully, my employer has been great in understanding my situation and has allowed me the time to make sure that proper healing has had a chance and I can return once I am ready, which thankfully is soon.

Ben's Insights

Many people who survive suicide find it hard to go to the same places they used to before, associate with the same people, and even work where they did prior to their attempt. Many find that making changes to their scenery is a coping mechanism to distance themselves from the triggers they'd had before. Others find that getting back to familiarity is the key to making sure things stay as normal as possible, making changes instead to just the factors that affected them before. Whatever method works for some might be different for others.

16—Don't Do What Ben Did

Throughout his story, Ben acknowledged and revealed some of the issues he'd been struggling with, some mistakes that he made, and many lessons he learned later, after reflecting on his actions. After sharing his story with me, I asked Ben the question: "Based on what you know now, what advice would you give someone in your shoes who is battling with depression and anxiety?" Ben was quick to reply with confidence what to tell readers NOT to do.

Please keep in mind that we are not medical professionals. You should consult with your personal physician to talk about a care plan to treat your personal situation or the situation of someone who may be suffering from depression.

As a summary, we came up with Ben's "Don't Do What I Did" List:

Ben's Top 5 DON'Ts

1. *Don't stop taking your medication abruptly, unless advised by your doctor*. Many medications need to be slowed down and tapered off in order to properly wean the body from the medication.

2. *Don't use alcohol while being treated for depression*. As mentioned in the book, alcohol in nature is a depressant, so it is not going to do you any favors in regards to getting better. You might think you need to drink to feel better, but in all essence, you are fueling the problem further.

3. *If what you are doing is NOT working, then don't keep doing it*. Talk to your doctor and be completely honest about your situation. They are there to help you, and there is no shame in asking for it. Remember, wanting to be better is a choice, but getting better likely involves receiving support from others.

4. *Don't isolate yourself from family or friends*. Dealing with this illness is something that many people are becoming more and more aware of, and sometimes, the best medicine is to deal with the situation head-on. Family and friends are in your life because they care,

not just part-time, but full-time. They can be a wonderful asset to have when combating depression, and nobody wants to fight it alone.

5. *Don't put on the mask.* It's natural to want to shield others from our pain and put on the happy face. This does not help anyone. Take a chance and connect with those you are comfortable with. It can also be helpful to talk with a complete stranger, such as a therapist. Working with a therapist should feel like what Ben described as talking with Kirk, whom he described as his late night bartender at the hospital. It can be liberating and will give you a new perspective. Be open and honest with what you are feeling so others can help.

Ben was open and honest, sharing everything he was feeling and the series of events that led him to attempt to take his life two different times. The story flows like a fiction novel, but it was real. He replayed the scenes and bared his soul within the pages of this book.

Since so few live to tell their story, it is difficult for friends and family members to understand what drives someone to take their own life or attempt suicide. It certainly seems to go against the grain of our strongest natural instincts, self-preservation and the will to live.

I don't believe that Ben wanted to die. He was looking for someone to intervene. He made several phone calls before his attempt on his life, and he ultimately called 911, the call that would save his life. Research has shown that most people who commit suicide do not want to die—they just want to stop hurting. Ben was in so much pain that he did not see any other way out.

I'll never forget our Monday morning staff meeting after the news spread that Ben had committed suicide over the weekend. The room was somber, the mood sad, and everyone was still in shock after learning what happened. At that time, we did not know if Ben was going to make it.

What was going through everyone's heads was simply—*how did we all miss the warning signs?* Many times, I have wondered, "What could I have done differently? Could we have intervened and changed the course?" The Ben we all knew would never have committed suicide. We were saddened and confused.

In the next chapter, we reflect on some of the suicide warning signs and touch on the topic of suicide prevention.

17—Suicide Warning Signs

If you have had had thoughts of suicide at some point in your life, even if it is a fleeting thought, you are not alone. I have read through Ben's story many times with different filters. All along, it is apparent that he tried to do the right things. He consulted with a medical doctor, sought out a therapist, and talked to a few close friends. He made attempts to change the course of his trajectory.

Emotional pain is a traumatizing and overwhelming experience, and it is hard for an outsider looking in to understand the crippling effect. Ben was blinded with hopelessness and despair. After reading his story, the patterns start to connect and warning signs emerge.

I have listed below the common warning signs from the National Suicide Prevention Lifeline's "Warning Signs" page (accessed November 18, 2015, www.suicidepreventionlifeline.org/learn/warni: gsigns.aspx). These are warning signs that may indicate someone is at risk for suicide.

If you or someone you know exhibits any of these signs, seek help as soon as possible by calling the Lifeline at **1-800-273-TALK** (8255).

Warning Signs

- Talking about wanting to die or to kill themselves
- Looking for a way to kill themselves, such as searching online or buying a gun
- Talking about feeling hopeless or having no reason to live
- Talking about feeling trapped or in unbearable pain
- Talking about being a burden to others
- Increasing the use of alcohol or drugs
- Acting anxious or agitated; behaving recklessly
- Sleeping too little or too much
- Withdrawing or isolating themselves

- Showing rage or talking about seeking revenge
- Displaying extreme mood swings

Armed with this information, it now becomes easier to identify the warning signs in Ben's story. His risk was augmented by his recent divorce, being underemployed, his sleeping difficulties, his increasing tendency to drink, his social withdrawal, and the fact that he had made a previous suicide attempt.

According to the American Foundation for Suicide Prevention, between 20–50% of people who commit suicide have tried before.

The most effective way to prevent suicide is to recognize the warning signs, respond immediately, and treat the underlying causes of the suicide, such as depression. It is not easy, but in the next chapter, we provide some guidance on how to be helpful to someone who is threatening suicide or is showing some of the warning signs.

18—Reach Out and Touch Someone

It is human nature to avoid something that makes us uncomfortable and uneasy. If you think someone that you care about is showing some of the suicide warning signs, the best advice that we can give is to take it seriously. Trust your instincts. *Should I say something? Or should I keep quiet about my concerns?* The answer is always—REACH OUT AND TOUCH SOMEONE who is struggling.

If you are unsure that someone is suicidal, the best way to find out is to start the conversation and ask. Showing someone that you care will not make them suicidal. Helpguide.org is an excellent website, full of information to help people who are suicidal or to help those who care for someone who may be contemplating suicide.

Here are some tips from this website's "Suicide Prevention" page (accessed on November 18, 2015, www.helpguide.org/articles/suicide-prevention/suicide-prevention-helping-someone-who-is-suicidal.htm).

How to start the conversation:

- I have been concerned about you lately.
- Recently, I noticed some difference in you and wondered how you are doing.
- I wanted to check in with you because you haven't seemed yourself lately.

Questions you can ask:

- When did you begin feeling like this?
- Did something happen that made you start feeling this way?
- How can I best support you right now?
- Have you thought about getting help?

What you can say that helps:

- You are not alone in this. I'm here for you.
- You may not believe it now, but the way you are feeling will change.

- I may not be able to understand exactly how you feel, but I care about you and want to help.
- When you want to give up, tell yourself you will hold off for just one more day, hour, minute—whatever you can manage.

Metanoia is an organization whose mission is to break down barriers that keep people from getting the help that they need.

Think about this statement taken from the article, "If You Are Thinking about Suicide ... Read This First," on Metanoia's site (accessed November 18, 2015, www.metanoia.org/suicide):

> *Suicide is not chosen; it happens when pain exceeds resources for coping with pain.*

The good news—it is possible to reduce the pain and find new ways to cope.

According to government suicide statistics, 70% of people who commit suicide tell someone about their plans or exhibit some of types of warning signs, like those discussed earlier.

Ben made several attempts to reach out to others to talk about his depression and what was going on inside his marriage. He even sought out a therapist after his first attempt at suicide. He began to talk about his depression with a few people close to him.

To most of the world, Ben hid his pain well. At work, Ben performed well and was well liked and respected by his peers and managers. His behavior was normal, and he was a fun guy to be around. His close family and friends, knowing he was going through some tough times, did try to intervene and offer solutions, but very few realized how serious his situation was.

Many would say the same thing about Robin Williams. He became skilled at hiding and masking the pain of depression through comedy. Sometimes people with depression are described as magicians. They are skilled at showing the happy side but may feel so alone and at a loss of how to find the help that they need. The good news is that depression can be treated, once it is correctly diagnosed. Realizing that you have a problem is the tricky part, but treatment is available.

Often, people dealing with depression try to cope in their own ways. Ben turned to alcohol to cope with the pain and depression. He had mood swings. He lost weight and talked about having trouble sleeping. Ben will be the first to tell you—

LISTEN, if what you are doing is not working, call in the experts. Help is available!

It is also hard to distinguish between someone with serious or severe depression with thoughts of suicide and someone who is just going through one of life's stressful situations—a death, divorce, work issues, relationship issues, etc.

I would say that I was in the same boat as a lot of people that knew Ben. Sure, Ben had some challenges and adversity going on in his life, but were they the sort of problems that would lead anyone to a suicide attempt? Most everyone was shocked to hear the news that Ben had attempted suicide.

Let's face it, depression is one of those conditions that is peculiar, mysterious, and makes us feel uncomfortable in knowing what to do or how to help a friend that we suspect is battling with it. The best course of action is to do everything in your power to get professional help for the person you care about. While you can't solve the problem or give advice on how to treat it, you can offer support and help the person locate a mental health professional, or take them to a doctor's appointment.

By starting the conversation, by taking a chance, you could open the doors to giving the person an opportunity to talk about feelings that can provide some release and comfort in knowing that they are not alone.

If you are like me, you are apt to say the wrong thing at the wrong moment. It is a touchy topic, and that is why it easier to not say anything. In Ben's case, I think everyone thought that whatever Ben was going though, it would pass. There is light at the end of the tunnel. Things will get better.

I have talked to Ben and to another suicide survivor when doing research for this book and have discovered there are things that you should *not* say or would *not* be very helpful to someone who has confided the following: "I want to kill myself," "My life is not worth living," or "I would be better off dead."

Read on. In the next chapter, we have listed the ten things *not* to say to a suicidal person.

19—Ten Things Not to Say

"I want to kill myself."

If you have ever heard these words from someone you care about, it almost pisses you off. You want to respond immediately and unleash all the reasons you can think of in the world why it is better to be alive than dead.

Remember that a person with depression may have clouded judgment. They obviously see and interpret reality in a different way. It is hard not to judge a person for thinking the way they do when they are suicidal.

Here we are sharing a from a great article, "10 Things Not to Say to a Suicidal Person" (Stacey Freedenthal, last modified March 3, 2015, www.speakingofsuicide.com/2015/03/03/what-not-to-say) from the site "Speaking of Suicide." Before you put your foot in your mouth, it is best to think before you say something that will close down the lines to communication.

Ten Things *Not* to Say

1. **"How could you think of suicide? Your life's not that bad."** Perhaps on the outside the suicidal person's life does not seem "that bad." The pain lies underneath. It can greatly help a suicidal person to feel understood. This sort of statement conveys disbelief and judgment, not understanding.

2. **"Don't you know I would be devastated if you killed yourself? How could you think of hurting me like that?"** Your loved one already feels awful. Heaping guilt on top of that is not going to help them feel soothed, understood, or welcome to tell you more.

3. **"Suicide is selfish."** This inspires more guilt. Two points are important here. One, many people who seriously consider suicide actually think they are burdening their family by staying alive. So, in their distressed, perhaps even mentally ill state of mind, they would be helping their loved ones by freeing them of this burden. Two, isn't it a natural response to excruciating pain to think

first of helping oneself escape the torment?

4. **"Suicide is cowardly."** This inspires shame. It also does not really make sense. Most people fear death. While I hesitate to call suicide brave or courageous, overcoming the fear of death does not strike me as cowardly, either.

5. **"You don't mean that. You don't really want to die."** Often said out of anxiety or fear, this message is invalidating and dismissive. Presume that the person really does mean that they want to die. It does more harm to dismiss someone who is truly suicidal than it does to take someone seriously who is not suicidal, so why not just take everyone seriously?

6. **"You have so much to live for."** In some contexts, this kind of statement might be a soothing reminder of abundance and hope. But for many people who think of suicide and do not at all feel they have much to live for, this remark can convey a profound lack of understanding.

7. **"Things could be worse."** Yes, things could be worse, but that knowledge does not inspire joy or hope. I compare it to two people who are stabbed, one in the

chest, one in the leg. It is far worse to be stabbed in the chest, but that does not make the pain go away for the person stabbed in the leg. It still hurts. A lot. So even if people who think of suicide have many good things going for them, even if their lives could be far worse, they still experience a seemingly intolerable situation that makes them want to die.

8. **"Other people have problems worse than you and they don't want to die."** True, and your loved one may well have already considered this with shame. People who want to die often compare themselves to others and come up wanting. They may even feel defective or broken. Comparing them to others who cope better may only worsen their self-condemnation.

9. **"Suicide is a permanent solution to a temporary problem."** I do know people, especially teens, for whom this statement was tremendously helpful. It spoke to them. But it also communicates that the person's problems are temporary when they might be anything but. In such a situation, a realistic goal for the person might be to learn to cope with problems and to live a meaningful life in spite of them. The other problem with this statement is it conveys that suicide is a solution—permanent, yes,

and a solution. At a minimum, I recommend changing the word "solution" to "act" or "action," simply to avoid reinforcing that suicide does indeed solve problems.

10. **"You will go to hell if you die by suicide."** Your loved one has likely already thought of this possibility. Maybe they do not believe in hell. Maybe they believe the god they believe in will forgive their suicide. Regardless, their wish to die remains. Telling them they will go to hell can exacerbate feelings of alienation.

There is so much information and great resources available on suicide and depression. We decided to list a resource section in the back of the book for some sites that Ben discovered through his journey of healing that were very helpful to him, and I also added a few sites that I came across that would be helpful to someone whose life has been touched by suicide in some manner.

I encourage anyone reading this story to read more books, do more research, read articles, and Google information on what you are seeking answers to. There are doctors, scholars, and scientists regularly writing and publishing new content on depression, anxiety, and other mental illnesses. If you seek, you will find something that makes sense in your situation and will give you a new idea, a new outlook, and new hope. The world is full of people who want to help. You task is to find them or ask a friend to help.

If you seek, you will find.

Before closing, Ben and I each want to share some final thoughts.

20—Ripple Effects

Final Thoughts from Shelia

Often it's the deepest pain which empowers you to grow into your highest self.
—Karen Salmansohn, healthplace.com

Ben's story has changed my life in a way that I was not expecting. All along, I'd thought we were writing this book to help others by exposing the down and dirty reality of suicide and depression, in hopes that we could save just one life and break down some of the social stigma around this topic. What I did not realize is that, in addition to this, I would be inspired by being connected and a part of Ben's story.

Over the past few months, since his suicide attempt, I have had the opportunity to reflect on the deep matters of life and death, and, like everyone else, I just wanted to make sense of this tragedy. It was not until I was writing this final chapter and reflecting on the story that I realized how my life had changed:

- I have become more compassionate to others who are struggling, not with just depression, but with other life struggles.
- I am more thankful and reflect more often on all the good things in my life.
- My goals are sharper and in clear focus.
- I have been inspired to read more books.
- I will be checking off a bucket list item. The experience of writing a book has opened new doors for me. I know I will write another book or two on other topics I am passionate about.
- I am grateful for my gift to see good in a tragedy, and I thank my parents for instilling this gift of a positive outlook.
- I feel more confident to take on new challenges. Life is too short to not take action.

Ben has already inspired me, and this book is not even published to the world at this moment in time—thank you Ben! There are ripple effects that are magical and unexpected when people connect and paths cross even for a brief period of time in the midst of tragedy. All lives matter, and we all have a unique gift to share.

Ben was given a second chance to rebuild and emerge into a greater version of himself. The rest of his story is yet to be written, but I think he will be successful and I think it will be a better story than this one. He has a long journey, but Ben is on the right path and has uncovered the secret key to rebuilding and changing his life—himself. The answers are deep inside. Through his healing, he has discovered more about himself. Along with a treatment plan, he is working on learning to love himself and that is where the real freedom lies.

My wish for Ben is to continue on the path of self-discovery and healing. It is difficult to see the good in tragedy when you are in the midst of adversity and life's challenges. Dig deeper. If we want to change the outcome of our life, we have to change the way we think and the way that we respond to life's events. It all comes from within.

I want Ben to be able to look back one day and say with confidence, "The best day in my life was the day I tried to take my life, and I was unsuccessful."

21—The Phoenix Rises

Final Thoughts from Ben

Like the mythical phoenix that rises from the ashes, my life has taken very much the same path. To say things have entirely changed wouldn't quite be a true statement, but they have improved. While my experiences that I've had in the now three months since I shot myself have shaped my life to come, they are something I wish I had never had to contend with to begin with.

Would I still be divorced? Unfortunately, yes. Am I still awaiting changes on the job front? Sure am. Am I living debt-free or without financial stress? Not hardly.

Well then, what has changed?

Plenty.

I have a newfound sense of self-worth, and my eyes have been opened to many things. I realize that I was obviously a prisoner of my own emotions, and there are many things I can now do to ensure that I keep that toll to a minimum going forward. Happiness is out there. I plan on finding it.

I have a wonderful network of friends that I can rely on to get me through tough times, and I've also developed a newfound friendship with myself. I am more aware of my limits and also not afraid anymore to ask for help if I need it. I'm following doctor's orders, keeping up on visits to ensure I'm healing properly, and concentrating on bettering myself in all areas.

There is promise on the horizon once again with work. I am even keeping in touch with Megan and Hunter. Things are going well so far in my life, and while nothing is done overnight, I have a clear and attainable set of goals and a timeline that isn't impossible to accomplish things.

I am keeping the terrible twins at bay the best I can. Depression and anxiety unfortunately will always be a part of my life. However, with the steps I'm taking and the path I'm following, they won't play too big of a part of it.

My story might be similar to many others who are suffering from this illness, and, if so, rest assured that you are not in the minority. Take it from someone who took things to the brink and lived to tell about it—I'd rather be around to make things right and enjoy another chance at everything important. Thankfully, I am alive to tell you this and am happy to be considered a cheerleader in your corner.

If you battle depression, you can heal from this. It takes time, commitment, and a lot of effort each day. If you are able to wake up knowing that the intention is to make the best day possible, trying to eliminate or not focus on negativity and make the positives a priority, you can lay your head on your pillow a little easier each night in your efforts to keep depression at bay.

Unfortunately there is no magic wand or specific treatment to cure this illness. My recommendations: self-reliance, practicing what works, and eliminating the things that don't make a great start to rising above it all—just like the phoenix.

A Request

Thank you for downloading this book and for taking the time to read! We really appreciate all of your feedback, and we love hearing what you have to say.

We would be very grateful and honored if you could take a few moments to leave us a helpful review on the book page on Amazon, letting us know what you thought of the book.

Thanks so much!

Ben & Shelia

Resources

National Suicide Prevention Lifeline

1–800–273–TALK

http://www.suicidepreventionlifeline.org

A free, 24–hour hotline available to anyone in suicidal crisis or emotional distress. Your call will be routed to the nearest crisis center to you.

Help Guide

www.helpguide.org/articles/suicide-prevention/suicide-prevention-helping-someone-who-is-suicidal.htm

This site is full of information to help people who are suicidal or to help those who care for someone who may be contemplating suicide. This specific page is well organized. It has a lot of information and provides links to other pages on the site as well as links to other sites.

Metanoia

www.metanoia.org/suicide/whattodo.htm

Here is a good article that outlines what you can do to help someone who is suicidal. Metanoia's mission is to break down barriers that keep people from getting the help that they need. Through communications, education, and advocacy, they work to make connections that can shed a little light.

Samaritans USA

www.samaritansusa.org

Samaritans centers provide volunteer-staffed hotlines and professional and volunteer-run public education programs, "suicide survivor" support groups, and many other crisis response, outreach, and advocacy activities.

Attempt Survivors

www.attemptsurvivors.com

This is a new blog for and by attempt survivors that was set up this year by the American Association of Suicidology. This is a good place to hear open, honest voices exploring life after a suicide attempt.

ULifeline

www.ulifeline.org/page/main/StudentLogin.htm

An anonymous online resource where you can learn about suicide prevention and campus-specific resources.

The Trevor Project

www.thetrevorproject.org/localresources

The Trevor Project is determined to end suicide among LGBTQ youth by providing life-saving and life-affirming resources, including a nationwide, 24/7 crisis intervention lifeline, a digital community, and advocacy/educational programs that create a safe, supportive, and positive environment for everyone.

YouSpoke

www.youspoke.org

YouSpoke is a nonprofit organization that cultivates a community for those deeply affected by suicide by offering them a creative outlet to share their stories.

Mental Health First Aid USA

www.mentalhealthfirstaid.org

This is a public education program that helps the public identify, understand, and respond to signs of mental illnesses and substance use disorders.

American Foundation for Suicide Prevention

www.afsp.org

This organization funds research, creates educational programs, advocates for public policy, and supports survivors of suicide loss. This websites contains a wealth of information and is easy to navigate. The site offers too many resources to mention, but it is well worth spending some time on it.

American Psychological Association

Suicide: What Therapists Need to Know

www.apa.org/education/ce/suicide.pdf

This is an excellent resource geared toward therapists, but that could help friends and family to understand what's going on. It discusses warning signs, assessment of the suicidal person, and treatment options, along with effective therapy approaches.

About the Authors

Ben Schwipps is an annuity marketing and service representative who has been in the insurance business for 16 years. He enjoys the challenges and constant changes that come with the annuity industry and the satisfaction of helping both the clients who buy them as well as the agents who sell them.

Ben currently lives in Osgood, Indiana. His spare times are spent with his children, fishing, buying cars (he's owned at least 108 so far), or enjoying Polaris RZR rides to off road destinations with friends.

Shelia Merkel is a senior operations manager who has 25 years of experience in building businesses and managing people. A serial entrepreneur, throughout her career she has launched or developed eight different service-related businesses. She has a passion for building teams and for helping employees grow and develop into their greatest potential in both their personal and professional lives.

Shelia currently lives in Cincinnati with her husband. In her spare time, she enjoys gardening, reading a good book, spending time with their two children, and taking Spyder bike rides with Hubby to explore new places with great local food.

Shelia's Story of This Book

I had always dreamed of writing a book about my culmination of business and professional experience and the many lessons learned from the school of hard knocks. Or perhaps I would write a book about growing up in a family of twelve. I never expected to help Ben write his story and publish a book in approximately 90 days. Literally, the day after I visited Ben in the hospital, I received an email that took me to the Self-Publishing School (SPS) website where I learned how to self-publish a book. I knew my story could wait. Ben's story needed to be written.

I am proud to be affiliated with SPS, so if you also have a dream to write a book and a story to be told, you too can make your dream a reality. Read on to learn more...

SELF-PUBLISHING
SCHOOL

NOW IT'S YOUR TURN

Discover the EXACT 3-step blueprint you need to become a bestselling author in 3 months.

Self-Publishing School helped us and now we want them to help you with this FREE VIDEO SERIES!

Even if you're busy, bad at writing, or don't know where to start, you CAN write a bestseller and build your best life.

With tools and experience across a variety niches and professions, Self-Publishing School is the only resource you need to take your book to the finish line!

DON'T WAIT

Watch this FREE VIDEO SERIES now, and say "YES" to becoming a bestseller:

https://xe172.isrefer.com/go/curcust/Smerkel

Made in United States
North Haven, CT
10 November 2026

22096539R00102